INTELLIGENCE

AND

NATIONAL ACHIEVEMENT

INTELLIGENCE
AND
NATIONAL ACHIEVEMENT

Editor
RAYMOND B. CATTELL

THE INSTITUTE FOR THE STUDY OF MAN INC.
Washington, D.C.

The Cliveden Press
Suite 520 1629 K Street, N.W.
Washington D.C. 20006

ISBN 0-941694-14-3

Manufactured in the United States of America

CONTENTS

INTRODUCTION:
The Contemporary Awakening

INTRODUCTION:
THE CONTEMPORARY AWAKENING

RAYMOND B. CATTELL
Distinguished Research Professor Emeritus
University of Illinois

Our society has been made aware in this decade that it is in trouble, educationally, economically, and in other ways. But like someone in a disturbing dream it is only vaguely aware of the real problem. Wishful thinking would tell us the problem is trivial and transient. My considered diagnosis is that we are in deeper trouble than we realize.

Someday there may be doctors of the health of societies, as we now have medical doctors for our personal health problems. To judge by the media the authorities accepted in this domain today are politicians, journalists, economists, bankers and so on. The intellectual bankruptcy of these is comically evident in, for example, their stock exchange predictions, their handling of the crime problem, and much else. There *is* an emerging class of true social scientists, though as yet with a limited science behind them, as represented by the present contributors and the many outstanding researchers they introduce. Someday the journalists and politicians will recognize that they deal with great complexities, beyond their training, and will erect the great social research institutions needed to monitor and cope with these problems.

Meanwhile the present little book, and others similarly concentrating scientifically on the functional life of society, may throw a few shafts of light to show the real depth of the problem. What has surfaced in the press at last is, first, an educational problem, documented as a decline of school standards since the early 1960s. This is analyzed here, beyond cavil, by Dr. Barbara Lerner. She shows the hollow facade of judging education by "years of school completed" and/or "degrees received" and introduces the technical advance of standard achievement test results, which show the U.S. (a) declining over most of 20 years, and (b) falling below Japan and Western European nations, so that "the only student groups whose test score means were usually lower. . .were those from underdeveloped nations." It is part of the illusion under which we have been living, and good proof of accommodation to permissiveness, that over these years the class grades have stayed up, but the real performance has gone down. Yet our simple minded belief in education in the abstract has stood up, for, as Dr. Lerner reports, "In the last two decades, we sent more of our young people to school for longer periods of time than any other nation in the world."

Dr. Lerner then logically moves from children at school to the economics of adults in jobs, and looks at the nation's "human capital," showing that economic forecasting of productivity is in part possible from achievement tests. As I write a copy of *Job Training News* comes on my desk with the heading "Good students become better soldiers." The connection of national earnings, national defense, adult literacy, and political intelligence with the level on the achievement tests Dr. Lerner describes is now shown by dozens of researches.

It is a weakness of human nature to cling to single causes for single effects, whereas a social scientist knows that his task is to give meaningful weights to multivariate causes. In my chapter here I have pointed out that the social psychologist now has a firm and widening basis of findings about scores on intelligence tests, personality tests, motivation tests and what I call "modulating situations" in society, as predictors of achievement, delinquency, mental illness and group behavior. Formulae and equations can be used, where presently politicians talk rhetoric and journalists talk banalities. However, on this particular matter of decline we are, as yet, starved of the research that would evaluate its roots. I will make an "educated guess," that the deterioration of performance is partly due to each of half a dozen factors, of which the three largest are (a) a decline in the innate intelligence level due to a century-long dysgenic situation, (b) a decline in morale, due to relativistic ethics, and permissiveness which has spread from society into its schools, and, (c) an increase in distractions through increased luxury, recreational time, and hours glued to TV shows.

Contributors here have mentioned but not documented the last. The fact that this cannot be our present focus does not mean that one should forget it. Elsewhere (1971) I have tackled it in depth; but the argument that the decline of morale, and the unwillingness to hold to standards, is basically due to the (legitimate) undermining of dogmatic, revealed religions by science is too unpleasant for many people to think about. I have suggested a solution, but meanwhile I will maintain that increases in crime and in diverse drug addictions, the decline of family influence, and the lack of seriousness in education will prove traceable to loss of authority in ethics, due to increasing scepticism concerning the "revealed," subjectively-based religions.

Better suited to examination in a book of this size is the first cause above – a possible genetic decline in intelligence. This has been a difficult idea for which to get popular acceptance, and the difficulty probably arises from three sources: (a) a reluctance by most people to believe that intelligence is substantially inherited, (b) justifiable doubts whether the effect of large family sizes of the less intelligent might not be offset by a lower marriage rate and a higher death rate among the subaverage, (c) the fact that the decline, which is very slow, is unlikely to be seen in personal experience, since most people move through life in intimate association mainly with their own age cohort.

The accumulating evidence that 60-80% of intelligence is genetic should end (a). It is about as heritable as stature. By shifting from a generation with poor nutrition to one very well fed we can get a shift of average stature from about 5 ft. 7 ins. to 5 ft. 9 ins., but you cannot go on doing this. And if you breed the next generation from the shorter members, then population stature, with the very best nutrition, will stay relatively low.

As to (b), my pioneer studies in 1935-37 showed that both in rural and urban areas decreasing intelligence steadily related itself to larger families – and did even when analyzed within one social status group. Furthermore culture-fair intelligence tests were used to clear up the question whether education rather than native intelligence might be the associate (Cattell, 1937). My calculation of an anticipated decline of average I.Q. of 1 point was checked by a new survey, after a 13-year lapse, in the same areas and schools, and no fall was found. (Contrary to the *rise* found on non-culture-fair tests). However, the fact that the intervening period was occupied by World War II and preparations for it, including migrations of workers, made the circumstances atypical and has prevented firm conclusions being drawn.

Since then intelligence and birth rate has been researched

four or five times, but as Dr. Vining points out, conclusions vary with situation, though in the main supportive of my first study, which was on a larger sample than some since. The failure of social scientists between 1937 and the present to execute the necessary large scale studies with appropriately adapted intelligence tests makes one wonder what subjects they have found more important than the intelligence of the nation, and all that depends on it. Into this neglected field comes now Dr. Vining, an unusual population specialist, who sees that it is perhaps inadequate to count heads without heeding what is inside them. With careful and sophisticated analyses he shows that, after most of 50 years since my study, much the same unfortunate relation exists between intelligence and family size. (Parenthetically let us remind the doubter of heredity that even if all the variance on intelligence were environment it would still be undesirable to have more children born into less cultured homes; for home is more important than school in fixing basic attitudes).

Dr. Lerner seems hopeful that changes in education will remedy the decline in achievements of which we are becoming aware, but realistically I cannot share that hope. I believe the changes she suggests should be put into effect; but we must have the courage to face the probability that the trouble goes deeper, and that more radical developments in public ideals, attitudes, and political action, are going to get to the real root of the trend, which lies in dysgenic birth rates.

As to the second component in educational decline – public morale – while we admitted above that its nature and causes are too subtle for easy analysis, and I resorted to reference to my special psychological study (1971), we can at least see it at a common experiential level in some comparisons of cultures and ethnic groups. In the state of Hawaii, where I happen to be writing, there are at least a dozen ethnic groups of good sample size and differing in racial composition and life style. The lack of seriousness about education, and lack of concern with conversations on things of the mind, can be well brought into relief by comparing some low groups (which shall be nameless) with say, high groups such as the Japanese, the Chinese, and the Jews, whose literacy, school achievement, and employment rates are high. One remedy that history tell us is effective for apathy in a country as a while, is outside challenge, and in this respect Sputnik was a blessing for American education.

When I became reasonably convinced in 1937 that there was a high probability of a slightly declining average intelligence in the population – incidentally at close to the rate Dr. Vining now calculates – I set out to ask what the consequences would be. The article I published in the *British Journal of Psychology* (1938) entitled "Some changes in social life in a community with a falling intelligence quotient" predicted five main effects: (a) a decline in educational performance, (b) an increase in the pool of permanently unemployed, containing many largely unemployable in a society of increasing technical complexity (Dr. Lerner's "structural unemployment"), (c) an increase in delinquency, with a fall of moral standards, since the greater part of crime, as in robbery and rape, is committed by persons of sub-average intelligence, (d) culturally a reduction of what can be defined as the "percolation range" of "civilized" ideas. The meaning of this is that although the media today are more active than formerly in putting out cultural news; there seems to be a limit to the percentage of the public penetrated by more realistically complex rather than simplistic ideas, (e) in politics and religion a tendency to rely on more traditional attitudes.

That the first of these has taken place is documented by Dr. Lerner. The second has reached the point where the alternative seems to be unemployment, or employment with inflation, through reduced efficiency. The third is evident, incidentally both in Europe and in the U.S.A., in crime statistics and the steady building of more prison accommodation. The fourth and fifth are harder to quantify and each reader will draw his own conclusions. I argued that those changes would be slow, and that with an accumulating compound interest, there would come a time – though quite a way off – when the magnitude would suddenly surprise us. I believe it would be little comfort to those – such as Leonard Darwin, Lord Horder, Sir Cyril Burt, Julian Huxley – who were with me in writing along these lines in the thirties, to have to say anything so fateful as: "We told you so." But if the hypothesis is that a fall of average intelligence and the resulting shifts in its distribution would, by the nature of intelligence and society, cause the above pattern of changes, then there is support for Dr. Vining's hypotheses and my own, based on family sizes, that a decline is in progress in this century. Probably, of course, like some long battle line, there is progress there and retreat here, in different ethnic groups, religions, and social classes. So vital a matter for the future of our country deserves research support about 100 times what it has had. Both Dr. Vining and I would readily admit that the dark sector in our survey has been the percent of unmarried persons, and of completely childless marriages, at various intelligence levels. Those figures, and the length of generations, death rates by intelligence, etc., urgently need investigation.

The link with natural survival that also needs investigation concerns firm data on the relation of individual achievement and intelligence to group performance, i.e. on the relation of mean population levels to levels of organized performance in the nation as a political-economic entity interacting with other such entities. We have data on small groups (Cattell & Stice, 1960) showing such cumulative effects of the characteristics of population members on total group performance, and Dr. Lerner's arguments are surely potent that the productivity and success of businesses is, as would be expected, partly a function of the competence of those in them. A nation is in many respects a large business and one can surely make, *a priori,* an extrapolation to their productivity and solvency. However, it is only in just the last decade that we have a thin harvest of direct evidence on this. The dimensions on which the chief (120) nations can factorially be measured and each given a syntality (corresponding to personality) *profile* have been discovered. One of them, for example, has to do with productivity, another with morale, and so on. If nations differ in the average intelligence levels of their populations, then correlations can be ascertained between each of the syntality dimensions and population intelligence. Population levels of intelligence would be likely to differ through selective migrations, e.g. the "brain drain" from Europe to the U.S. after the war, and through the strength of eugenic and dysgenic internal processes, and test samples suggest that real differences in the mean I.Q. *do* exist. As I show in my concluding article here, though the national differences of mean level (from Buj's appreciable samples measured with culture-fair intelligence texts) are small, yet a significant correlation with productivity is found for the mean population intelligence levels. Incidentally one would expect most effect on both productivity and potency of national defense to derive from the magnitude of the supply *in the topmost ranges* of intelligence, from which, given appropriately more advanced education, resourceful management and beneficial invention result. The numbers in that range depend both on their birth rates and the assortiveness of mating, and a rise in the latter could admittedly *temporarily* offset a decline in the former. Surely *everyone* will agree that the schools should turn to giving appropriate education to these much brighter individuals, but it will take *a more far-sighted public* to encourage measures for their greater production.

INTELLIGENCE AND NATIONAL ACHIEVEMENT

THE ROLE OF PSYCHOLOGICAL TESTING IN EDUCATIONAL PERFORMANCE: THE VALIDITY AND USE OF ABILITY PREDICTIONS

RAYMOND B. CATTELL
Distinguished Research Professor Emeritus
University of Illinois

1. History of the Application of Psychological Tests in Schools to Present Date

Anyone who wishes to delve into the first historical glimmerings of practical work on individual differences in ability will need to look back to the work of Sir Francis Galton and of Professor McKeen Cattell towards the end of the last century. Sir Francis Galton was interested particularly in reaction times, goodness of memory, and so on, and accumulated some norms for the general population. McKeen Cattell took a wider span of abilities and was interested to find out what underlying basic abilities were projected into actual performances. Unfortunately, the methods used (1901) did not permit a solution at that time. Sir Francis Galton's work (1883) was very fruitful, however, in that it led, among other things, to the recognition that human traits tended to be *normally* distributed and it led also to the development of the correlation coefficient for determining how much any two abilities are related.

At the turn of the century, interest in intelligence grew rapidly, partly because the schools were concerned to separate out those who were merely retarded in their school performance from those who were mentally defective. Indeed, this was the situation which led to Afred Binet being instructed by the school authorities in Paris to develop an intelligence test. We shall see soon that the development of intelligence tests took two quite distinct paths: one more theoretically based; and one more quickly adapted to the needs of applied psychology. In England, Spearman (1904, 1923) and Karl Pearson (1904) as well as Cyril Burt (1925) became interested in the more theoretical approach which finally expressed itself in Spearman's conception of a single general factor. This general factor was theorized to be a broad ability that runs through all cognitive performances, and it would require that the different kinds of ability measurements be substantially positively correlated. It so happened that the theoretical approach and the practical one started off together, as if at the crack of a pistol. Spearman's article (1904) "General intelligence objectively determined and measured" and the actual intelligence test put together by Binet and Simon (1905) were within a year of each other.

The approach of Binet proceeded by common sense observations, especially in America, in a relatively theoryless fashion, stringing together a variety of performances that one felt *should* be representative of intelligence. There were, of course, *some* theoretical concepts in this work. For example, those dealing with backward children defined intelligence as "the ability to think abstractly" (Burt, 1961) because the mental defective could often still handle concrete things but not abstractions. Teachers generally, of course, thought of intelligence as the "capacity to learn," and this finished up in the refined definition that "intelligence is the capacity to acquire capacity." There was yet a third source of observation leading to theories, namely, the observation of the ability of animals of different levels of evolution to solve problems. From this emerged the definition that "intelligence is adaptability to new situations."

The approach begun by Binet and Simon (1905) quickly resulted in translations of the test into English in England, and into the Stanford Binet test in America, and so on to a variety of tests in a direction of movement in which the WISC (See Cattell and Johnson, 1983) and the WAIS (Wechsler, 1958) are the present day representatives. On the other hand, the approach begun by Spearman developed powerfully into theoretical forms and statistical-mathematical models that have been extremely valuable not only in the advance of ability testing, but also in other fields of investigation of psychological trait structure generally.

Spearman introduced the method of factor analysis in which one takes perhaps 30 or 40 variables and correlates them over perhaps 200 or 300 people and then looks at the correlations to see what underlying influences can be expected to be active in producing those correlations. This was aided by several mathematicians, such as Jacobi and Hotelling, and issued ultimately in what is called multifactor analysis, for which Thurstone (1937) in Chicago was responsible in its most developed form. The theory of abilities now became a science rather than a matter for conjecture and for shaping by the rather blind and blundering methods of intuition. Spearman claimed that a single general factor underlaid most cognitive abilities and that it was "loaded" more highly in abstract matters such as analogies, classifications, choosing exact synonyms, and putting spatial puzzles together. Thus he was able for the first time to apply an objective test of the *validity* of any given intelligence test. Its validity would be the extent to which it correlated with an expressed general factor which could be defined from a broad array of the highly loaded abilities.

This matter we can follow up more intensively in the next section, but, meanwhile, we should glance at the effect that these developments had on the use of tests in schools. An increasing use of intelligence tests, particularly in schools and industry and other fields, is associated particularly with the name of Sir Cyril Burt in England (1917), of Binet in France (1905), of Stern in Germany (1922), and of Terman in America (1926). The Binet, as an individual test, became much used also in the offices of psychiatrists and medical doctors, the latter being in most school systems used by the professionals who were responsible for assigning backward children to specially adapted schools. Soon after tests came in use for children of various ages, Stern, in Germany, pointed out that if one divided what he called the mental age by the actual age of a child one attained what he called an *intelligence quotient* and that this intelligence quotient remained essentially constant over the years of the child's development. This tended to be interpreted as meaning that the I.Q. measured a relatively innate general ability, but in a strictly logical approach one could account for it both as due to heredity and as due to a uniformity of the lives of most children in relation to school experience, as they grew up.

On this general assumption intelligence tests began to be used for scholarship selection in the 1920s; and Sir Cyril Burt in London, in particular, developed a refined and sophisticated system whereby through intelligence tests taken at 11 years of age, children were set in different streams of educational intensity suited to their natural capacities. This endured for 20 years, with general satisfaction, but as we shall see in Section 8, it came under considerable debate in the 1950s and for political and other reasons has tended to be abandoned in some of the countries that accepted this design. Whatever we may say later about this complex issue, the fact is that an individual's I.Q.

measurement has about a 50/50 chance of staying within plus or minus 5 points of the original measurement when a child is retested after a year or two. Thus one can say that in roughly the first half of this century there was a steady and rapid increase in use of intelligence tests in the schools, followed and accompanied also by tests of other special mental abilities; but that, partly through abuses and partly through inherent inadequacies of understanding by psychologists, the use suffered some setbacks in the 1960s and 1970s.

2. History of Development of Research Concepts About the Measurements of Human Abilities and the Definition and Validation of Intelligence Measurement

As seen above the second, relatively theoryless, approach to intelligence and ability testing ultimately came to grief, as any one familiar with the history of science might expect. Without factor analysis and similar correlational methods there was nothing to prevent anyone setting up his own definition of intelligence, and there were not lacking many psychologists happy to put forward such subjective definitions (Terman, 1926) (Wechsler, 1958). The inevitable result in fact was that the only definition that could be agreed upon in the tradition of the Binet and the WAIS was that "intelligence is what intelligence tests measure!" It then became almost a commercial matter, of good advertising, to convince psychologists what particular intelligence tests best measured intelligence.

On the other hand, Spearman (1905, 1923) and Burt (1940), showed that the general factor obtainable from a correlation matrix could be uniquely determined and defined. And although this was debated for some years, e.g. by Sir Godfrey Thomson (1939), it became in the end generally accepted that if the general factor *could* be located it would be *uniquely* located. While the theory of *g* was thus crystallizing, Thurstone, at Chicago, went off in a new direction to look for what are now called the *primary mental abilities* (1938). He showed that one could locate functional unities also at a different level from *g* among the many cognitive tests that were used, such as spatial ability, verbal ability, numerical ability, inferential reasoning, inductive reasoning, perceptual speed, and so on. On seeing this evidence for distinct primary abilities a lot of psychologists followed their usual habit of jumping hastily upon a promising looking bandwagon, and announced that the theory of *g* was no longer of any importance and that one should throw away I.Q. tests and now measure only these special primary abilities.

However, both Thurstone himself and the present writer (1941) showed that, by what is called a second order factor analysis, one could still find Spearman's *g* as it were "hiding in back" of these primary abilities. For example, one visible consequence in experimental results is that verbal and other primaries are positively correlated. The explanation of how this structure came about was not clear and is still not fully clear today. One possibility is that the general intelligence becomes practiced more in some fields than others with each individual, and that if he has a lot of practice in reading, for example, he will develop a high degree of verbal ability. On the other hand there is an equally tenable theory, for which there is some recent support, that the primary abilities represent hereditary differences. For example, women are higher than men on verbal ability at every age from infancy and, conversely, men are higher than women on the spatial ability. Even where there is some equality of training the difference seens to hold, as instanced in the fact that girl babies learn to speak significantly earlier than boy babies.

The nature of the primary abilities was thus first discovered in the 1930s and became well confirmed and precisioned in the next decade. A third development in knowledge of structure then occurred, beginning in the 40s (Cattell, 1943) and reaching some precision in the 60s. Therein Spearman's *g* was found to split, by more precise factor analytic methods, into *two distinct g's* which have been called g_f, fluid intelligence, and g_c, crystalized intelligence. The differences of these two kinds of ability (Cattell, 1963, 1971; Horn & Cattell, 1966) are several, as follows:

1) Fluid intelligence is involved in tests that have very little cultural content, whereas crystallized intelligence loads abilities that have obviously been acquired, such as verbal and numerical ability, mechanical aptitude, social skills, and so on.
2) The age curve of these two abilities is quite different. They both increase up to the age of about 15 or 16, and slighly thereafter, to the early 20s perhaps. But thereafter fluid intelligence steadily declines whereas crystallized intelligence stays high. (Horn & Cattell, 1966).

3) The standard deviation of intelligence quotients is about 15 points of I.Q. with crystallized intelligence but is about 23 or 24 points of I.Q. with fluid intelligence.

4) There is some evidence that brain damage affects fluid intelligence no matter what the damage area is in the brain, and roughly in proportion to the extent of the damage; whereas crystallized intelligence may be affected in a more local way as when a person loses the ability to handle words in aphasia but can still handle spatial problems. (Lashley, 1963; Reitan, 1959).

5) There are indications that fluid intelligence has a higher degree of heritability than crystallized intelligence and indeed some of the debates and misunderstandings on the inheritance question probably derive from the debaters unwittingly talking about different intelligences.

In regard to the third of the above differences, it has been speculated that educational customs have a good deal to do with it. In effect it means that if children are kept in locked step, according to age, in classrooms, the less bright are pressured to advance more in crystallized intelligence and the more bright – that is to say those highest on fluid intelligence – are caused to mark time, perhaps becoming bored, and thus not advancing in crystallized intelligence as much as would be expected from their fluid intelligence. This fits in with the broad theory of "investment" (Cattell, 1971: Horn & Cattell, 1966), according to which crystallized intelligence is the result of the investment of fluid intelligence in those more complex fields of discrimination in every day matters in which intelligence would be helpful.

While work was going steadily ahead by quantitative and statistical methods, clarifying the structure of abilities in terms of primary abilities; of second order general factors; and of the important differences of fluid and crystallized intelligence, work in a more qualitative form was going ahead under such psychologists as Piaget (1960) who recognized in young children that certain solutions to problems were often generalized to give an immediate step-up in the solution of a fairly wide array of abilities, associated with a particular concept. This could well be the basis of the primary abilities; and what has been called the "triadic theory" of ability structure (Cattell, 1971), in fact recognizes three tiers in ability structure: the *primaries* or "aids" corresponding to the Piaget notions; the *provincial* broader abilities which are associated with the special senses, such as auditory ability and visualization; and finally, the truly *general* abilities such as fluid and crystallized intelligence, immediate memory, perceptual speed, etc.

While this advance in the theory of ability structures was going on, interest arose in the physiological concomitants. Of course these could not be investigated insightfully until the ability structure itself, as emerging in actual behavior, became established. But Lashley (1963) produced much evidence from animal work that general intelligence was positively related to the size and the weight of the cortex, and even among humans there is still some positive correlation, though very small, between outer head size and intelligence. It remains to be seen whether when cortical volume is measured more precisely by x-rays, etc. this correlation rises at all. On the physiological side, it is recognized that temporary states of oxygen deficiency, etc. will lower intelligence test performance and that certain physiological deficiencies will cause mental defect to the point of imbecility. The use of primary ability tests and tests of the provincials also has helped a good deal in brain surgery in locating areas of damage. Thus, in summary, as of 1980 a good deal has become known scientifically about the nature and measurement of human abilities. For example, we have the triadic structure of abilities, the degrees of heritability, the fact that intelligence in normally distributed in most populations, the fact that there is no sex difference on intelligence as a whole, the fact that age curve development follows a different form in fluid and crystallized intelligence, and the fact that learning in various domains is positively correlated with performance on intelligence tests.

3. The Effectiveness of Mental Tests in the Schools Psychologists's Task of Diagnosing Retardation, Educational Difficulties, and Scholarship Capacity

As we turn to applications we noted that a rule of thumb use of tests has proceeded alongside the more sophisticated use now possible from knowledge of the structure and the developmental properties of abilities, as discussed above. In the first place the construction of the most valid intelligence tests has profited from the knowledge of structure. For example, it is known that tests which involve what Spearman defined as "the perception and eduction of relations and correlates" is central to a good intelligence sub-test. Thus in the case of the analogies test where we might way:

"kitten is to cat as puppy is to _____"

one first educes a relation between kitten and cat, namely a generational relation, and then having educed that relation one applies it to puppy producing the correlate "dog."

This process of perceiving relationships enters also, of course, into classification tests, e.g., "Point out the odd item in:

Beech Oak Grass Ash"

The same theory of intelligence, defining it as the capacity to perceive complex relations, shows that we should be able to test intelligence by complex relations among spatial and auditory presentations *that have no "reference meaning," in the sense of not requiring prior knowledge about them.* Thus the five subtest examples in Figure 1 do not depend on knowledge and show what can be done to produce culture fair tests.

These examples show that it should be possible to set up a culture fair intelligence test with purely "perceptual" items. When this is done the factor analyses (Cattell, 1971) show that such tests are good measures of fluid intelligence rather than crystallized intelligence, which latter is the main factor measured in the WAIS, the Binet, the Stanford, and other traditional tests (Cohen, 1959).

That these tests can, in social use, be considered culture fair is shown by two findings: 1) That immigrants to the U.S. from a different culture tested on arrival and tested a year or so later rise considerably on ordinary intelligence tests but do not do so on a culture fair intelligence test (Cattell, Feingold and Sarason, 1981). 2) When *identically the same tests forms* are given in different countries they give mean values for the populations that are virtually equal. This has been shown for example, to hold for the U.S.A., Hong Kong, Japan, Italy, Germany, and so on.

The first use of intelligence tests in school systems, as indicated above in introducing the Binet, was in the form of *individual tests,* for the clinical purpose of picking out defectives. The points of separation have been at I.Q.'s of 70, 50, and 25, but with changing labels. The original labels at the beginning of

FIGURE 1

Examples of Five Culture Fair Perceptual, Relation-Education Subtests of Proven Validity for Fluid Intelligence

Choose one to fill dotted square.

Series

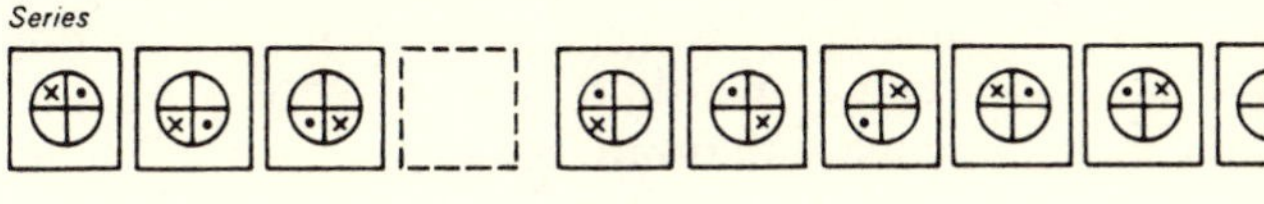

Choose odd one.

Classification

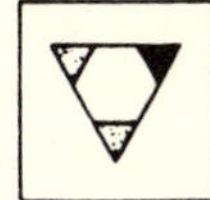 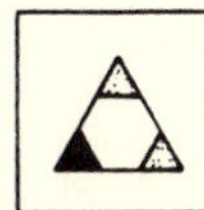 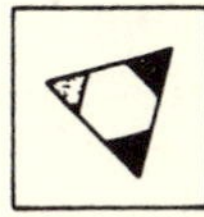 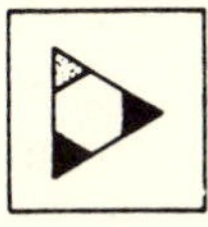 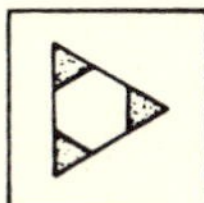

Choose one wherein dot could be placed as in item on left.

Topology

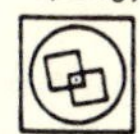 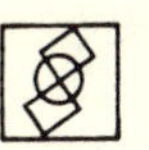 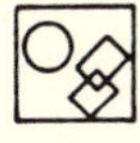   

Choose one to complete analogy.

Analogies

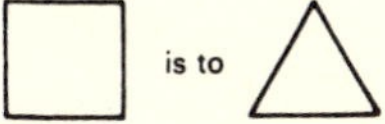

as

is to

 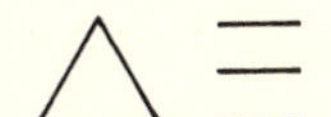

Choose one to fill empty square at left.

Matrices

 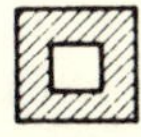  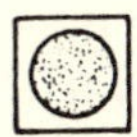   

From Form B, Scales II and III, IPAT Culture-Fair Test. By kind permission of the Institute of Personality and Ability Testing, 1602 Coronado Drive, Champaign, Illinois

Analogies section from Cattell Scale II, Harrap & Co.

the century were the idiot level at an I.Q. below about 25, the imbecile below an I.Q. of about 50, and the mental defective below a figure of 70. These standards have not changed but the labels have, in what is probably an ineffectual attempt by euphemisms to escape from the social recognition of serious retardation involved in applying these terms. In any case, the important outcome was that the introduction of intelligence tests enabled the diagnosis to be much more reliably made. The present writer can remember in the 1920s seeing school medical officers who would point to a picture of Queen Victoria on the wall and ask the child who it was. After 2 or 3 questions of that kind the doctor would pronounce the child normal or mentally defective.

A very common use in Child Guidance Clinics and the like became, and still is, that of separating low intelligence from poor school performance. There are many causes, such as absence from school through illness, parents who move around too frequently, and so on, which produce educational backwardness in children of quite normal intelligence. Using both standardized school achievement measures and intelligence tests, as well perhaps as primary ability tests, a good psychologist today can easily distinguish what the child's problem is and arrange remedial education on the one hand or allocation to a special school on the other.

The second main use of ability tests in the school system has been in connection with promotion and scholarship selection. As stated above, this has in the last two decades been under debate, and we shall probe the matter more fully later. Meanwhile we are concerned only with the extent of experience with the methods and their degree of success. It would take too much space to set out data from different countries on this matter but it can be said definitely that it has been a considerable success in as much as a child's performance 2, 3, and 4 years ahead is better predicted by an intelligence test than by his momentary examination grade levels at the time. The results of practice with tests of this kind, statistically analyzed, is that university students average higher on the intelligence quotient than those who do not go to the university, and in schools like those of England, Germany, and France in the last generation, the children who went to selective secondary schools proved higher in average intelligence than those who did not. The following Figure 2, shows results from England:

FIGURE 2

Ranges of Intelligence in English Schools and Universities

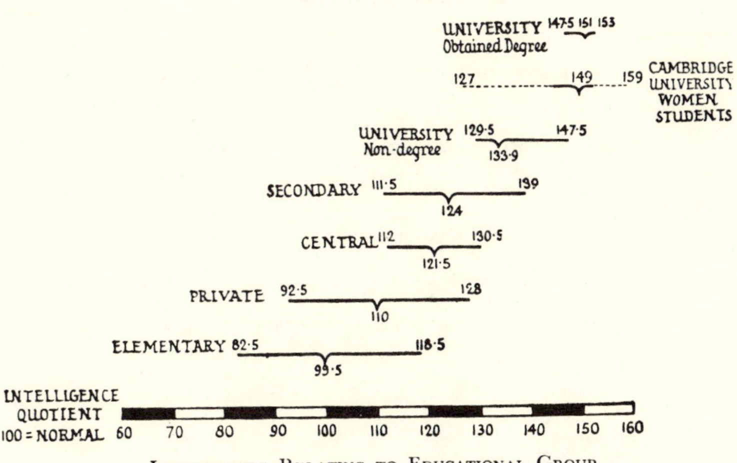

INTELLIGENCE RELATING TO EDUCATIONAL GROUP

A third main area of use of ability tests in schools is that of vocational guidance or counseling. Of course ability tests are also used from the opposite end of the employment transaction in vocational selection by industries and the military. Again the success of this practical application has been very great.

Probably the best and most systematic evidence on what is gained from the use of psychological tests in regard to occupations is available in the records of the military psychologists in World Wars I and II. In World War I there was only a rough beginning, but in World War II psychological testing units were installed in the Army, the Air Force and the Navy. Selection for special training for officer candidate schools, for medical training, etc. was carried out with ever more advanced methods. Table One shows some results from Harrell and Harrell (1945) on the average intelligence levels found for various occupations.

Similar results were obtained in England for occupations in peace time by the present writer as shown in Figure 3.

There should be no mistaking of the fact that although there are significant differences in the mean I.Q. between, say, janitors and doctors, there is nevertheless a wide spread in each

TABLE 1

Occupational Means of Intelligence Based Partly on Army Drafts (American Data & English Data)

Distribution of Intelligence Over Occupations

Occupation	*Mean*
Professors and Researchers	134 (C1)
Professors and Researchers	131 (C2)
Physicians and Surgeons	128 (C1)
Lawyers	128 (H&H)
Engineers (Civil and Mechanical)	125 (C1)
School Teachers	123 (C)
School Teachers	123 (H&H)
School Teachers	121 (H&W)
General Managers in Business	122 (C)
Educational Administrators	122 (C)
Pharmacists	120 (H&H)
Accountants	119 (C)
Accountants	128 (H&H)
Nurses	119 (C1)
Stenographers	118 (C)
Stenographers	121 (H&H)
Efficiency (Time Engineer) Specialists	118 (C)
Senior Clerks	118 (C)
Managers, Production	118 (H&H)
Managers, Miscellaneous	116 (H&H)
Cashiers	116 (H&H)
Airmen (USAF)	115 (H&H)
Foremen (Industry)	114 (C)
Foremen	109 (H&H)
Telephone Operators	112 (C)
Clerks	112 (C)
Clerks, General	118 (H&H)
Salesmen (Traveling)	112 (C)
Salesmen (Door to Door)	108 (C)
Salesmen	114 (H&H)
Psychiatric Aides	111 (C&S)
Electricians	109 (H&H)
Policemen	108 (C)
Fitters (Precision)	108 (C1)
Fitters	98 (H&W)
Mechanics	106 (H&H)
Machine Operators	105 (H&H)
Store Managers	103 (C)
Shopkeepers	103 (H&W)
Upholsterers	103 (H&H)
Butchers	103 (H&H)
Welders	102 (H&H)
Sheet Metal Workers	100 (C)

Combined results on occupation means from Cattell (C, C_1, C_2) (1934), Harrell and Harrell (Harell (1945), Himmelweit and Whitfield (H & W) (1944) and Cattell and Shotwell (C & S) (1954).

FIGURE 3

Occupation Ranges of Intelligence (English Data)

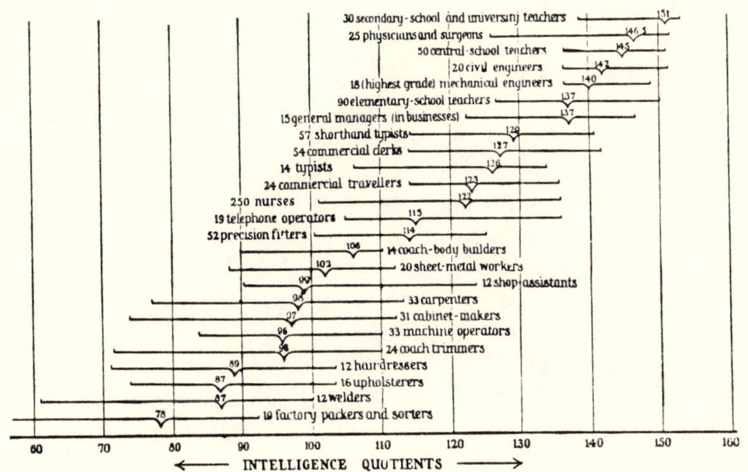

Intelligence Levels in Various Occupations (For Purposes of Vocational Guidance)

The central figure and ⌄ on each line indicates the average I.Q. for the sample taken. The length of the line subtends the scatter of I.Q. for the middle 50 per cent. in that occupation.

Abstracted from measurements on more than a thousand adults, as reported in "Occupational Norms of Intelligence and Standardisation of an Adult Intelligence Test," by R. B. Cattell, *Brit. J. Psychol.*, vol. xxv, July 1934.

Further data contributing to the standardisation of occupational norms of I.Q. will be found in "Mean Intelligence Scores of a Random Sample of Occupations," by H. T. Himmelweit and J. W. Whitfield, *J. Indus. Medicine*, 1226, 1944 :.

occupation. This could be due on the one hand to the fact that as the Old Testament says "chance happeneth to them all." But, although there is no question that accidents of life and background play a large role in where one finishes up occupationally, the spread in real effectiveness need not be as big as these diagrams suggest. The total effectiveness of the individual is not just his or her intelligence, but also depends on a number of character qualities and it is quite likely that if one took a combination of intelligence and the necessary character qualities one would find less spread within each occupation, relative to the difference between them, than is evidenced in the above diagrams.

In some school systems one has already before school leaving a sorting which is half way towards an occupational sorting. For example, in the British schools in the first half of this century it was usual for the higher secondary and public schools to lead to the professions, for the intermediate schools to lead to clerical and similiar skilled occupations, and for the elementary schools in the main to lead to semi-skilled and unskilled occupations – and the curricula were adapted to this. Clearly, this presupposed that the selection by abilities that was going on was adequate to be a basis for such predictions (Burt, 1917, 1959) but as we shall argue in Section 7 below, selection by personality and motivation measures is also necessary if one is to achieve predictions of future performance that are better than those by abilities alone.

4. The Use of Tests in Child Guidance Clinics, Handling Problem Behavior in School

A curious fact of clinical practice is that it has been usual to give ability tests to problem children, neurotic children, and the like, brought to Child Guidance Clinics, but not to adults who visit a psychotherapist or a psychiatrist. For example, one can read Freud from end to end without encountering any case in which an intelligence test was applied. To some extent this represents nothing but blind tradition, but it also has some basis in the fact that problem behavior in school, which at first sight seems to be emotional in nature, often turns out to be tied up with ability and performance difficulties. At the same time, in passing, it might be suggested that more direct investigation of personality *dynamics* might well be undertaken with children with school problems, and conversely, some measures of ability taken on the adult patients who go to a psychotherapist. For it is quite possible that some of the difficuties of the adult arise from inability to keep up with his professional or work demands, or from lack of skills, e.g., in dealing with people, in his everyday life. However, our concern now is with the use of ability tests only in Child Guidance Clinics. The actual practice of ability testing in Child Guidance Clinics has shown some ingenious developments in finding the kinds of tests that children of short attention capacity and unusual educational backgrounds can best show their abilities in. For example, quite a variety of form boards, such as the Seguin, were introduced permitting manipulative activity which held the attention of a child who might not concentrate well on pencil and paper tests. Here also came the Healy picture completion tests, the Gesell three figure board, and the Glueck ship test. There were also other tests which drew on other abilities such as the Goodenough drawing of a man test and the Knox cube and others. It was not unusual also to apply tests of sensory acuity, as of hearing and vision, since every now and then some child would be considered mentally defective who was actually almost deaf. As primary ability tests appeared, such as those of Thurstone, it also was more usual in special cases to go beyond intelligence to the primary abilities. For referrals from the classroom would often include a statement that the child seemed unable to spell or to visualize forms of figures and so on. Again, research findings on the structure of abilities became important. For example, it has not been unusual for a teacher to conclude that a child who couldn't spell must be unintelligent, but Thurstone's work showed virtually zero correlation between general intelligence and ability to spell, and, indeed, I have encountered in one or two leading executives in big business a marked inability to spell.

As stated above, the reason for the need for a thorough ability battery to be applied in Child Guidance Clinics is that scholastic disabilities and emotional and behavioral problems seem intimately intermingled in this age range. This was first brought out in two classical books by Burt, namely, *The Young Delinquent* (1935) and *The Backward Child* (1937). It was soon noted, for example, both in London by Burt, and in Chicago by Healy, that young delinquents on the whole average distinctly below par in intelligence. This does not hold in all societies and at all ages, and indeed the relation tends to disappear in the adult realm, but it is evident that some forms of simple delinquency are associated with poor mental capacity.

In most Child Guidance Clinics the referrals from schools for study by the psychologist, are about 50/50 of cases of backwardness and cases of problem behavior. It soon became an adage in Child Guidance Clinics that "scratch a case of scholastic backwardness and you find a case of emotional problem behavior." It is true that perhaps a half of all cases referred for backwardness turned out to be cases where the school performance was proportional to what one would expect from the intelligence score and the intelligence score was distinctly low. Another half of the cases, approximately, however, would show a perfectly normal or even superior intelligence associated with backwardness in school achievement. Moreover, every now and then, one would encounter a child with an I.Q., for example, of 130, or even higher, who for various emotional reasons detested school and played truant. Sometimes it was as simple as that he was bored by the average pace of the class and became increasingly inattentive and day dreaming. In other cases, of course, there were home background difficulties and the Clinic operated through social workers to try to produce situational changes that would result in better school achievement more in line with the individual's proven intelligence. In passing, one may note that the use of individual intelligence and ability testing, e.g., as by use of the Stanford, Binet, or the WISC in Child Guidance Clinics in counseling resulted in the view that individual testing is more reliable than group testing. This created a suspicion of group testing which is in fact unjustified. If properly proctored, assuring that every child is attending to the instructions and timing, there are actually some *advantages* in group testing. For example, a child will often be shy and awkward in an individual testing situation, showing poor results in consequence of his embarrassment, and, on the psychologist's side there is a tendency to give a bright-looking child the benefit of the doubt on one or two ambiguous responses. If properly carried out with a well-designed intelligence test, group testing can be depended upon to be reliable for the great majority. In any case, a repeat testing 2 or 3 days later, will often reveal any inaccuracies by showing an undue discrepancy between the first and second performance.

5. The Correlation Magnitudes Typically Reached Between School Performance and Psychological Tests

The word prediction has two meanings in psychological research: 1) the estimation of a performance A from a performance B at some given time, 2) the more common dictionary meaning of estimating from some performance today what the performance will be, say, a year or more hence. Much psychological data that is published concerns itself only with the first of these as in, for example, the extent to which the intelligences of 200 children in March will predict the scholastic performances in the same month. However, psychology becomes a superior science when it can also predict into the future as when one is selecting, say, scholarship children for special advanced education which leads to going to college in the future. The difference between the two capacities to predict is the difference between mere statistics on the one hand, and the science of psychology on the other, which knows what the typical age development changes are or, what traits are more hereditary than others, and what situations will modify traits. An illustration of the difference of these two could be given by considering the testing of draftees into the military, say at an age of about 20. If we were out to estimate what these draftees would do in ordinary schooling, immediately, an ordinary, traditional intelligence test, which tests crystallized intelligence, would do slightly better than a culture fair intelligence test. The correlation of the crystallized intelligence test with present learning level in classrooms is, as we shall see below, about 0.5 to 0.6, whereas the prediction from a culture fair test is more likely to be between 0.4 and 0.5. The reason for the difference in this case is that the traditional intelligence tests already contains in the crystallized discriminatory habits which it tests *a good deal that is in fact school achievement itself.* Thus one is predicting school achievement not only from intelligence but from a mixture of school achievement *itself* with the intelligence test scores. But now let us consider that these recruits go into quite different performances from anything to which they are accustomed, in handling shall we say planes and machine guns rather than English and arithmetic tests. In this case the culture fair test gives a much better prediction, because it tells us how the person will adapt to an entirely new type of material, in terms of his relationship-perceiving capacity. In the case of the traditional intelligence test the prediction will be biased by inclusion of the level of certain classroom skills which have no relevance whatever to the new world into which the recruit moves.

The level of prediction of school achievement (average over subjects) from the ordinary intelligence test is known from literally hundreds of research studies to be about +0.55. That is to say, the correlation of the intelligence test with the school grades would be about .55. It will be higher or lower according to certain circumstances, as follows. First, it will depend on reliability of the intelligence test on the one hand and the reliability of school grading system on the other. If external examinations such as those set up by the Educational Testing Service are used instead of a teacher's classroom grades one usually gets somewhat higher figures. Most intelligence tests that take up to three quarters of an hour or an hour achieve about as much as can be achieved in terms of reliability – though by no means always in validity. So not much improvement arises from applying what is called the "correction for attenuation" for unreliability in the intelligence test itself. Probably the predictive correlation, with perfectly reliable tests, is going to center on about .6.

A second factor which influences the degree of correlation between school performance and the intelligence test is the range of intelligence and of achievement in the given neighborhood or school. The greater the range the larger the correlation coefficient. Thus in college freshmen, who have already been restricted in range to some extent in regard to both intelligence and achievement, the correlations are likely to fall to about .4.

The third, and some would think the most important, factor is the students' uniformity of exposure to educational conditions in the school and in the home. Where these conditions are highly uniform as in the middle class environment where schools are good and the home backgrounds are stimulating, the correlation is likely to be better than in neighborhoods where school achievement is determined more by other influences than the individual's ability.

As indicated above, the prediction from intelligence tests depends also on the kind of school achievement that is being measured. Each subject has what is called a *g*-saturation which is usually determined by correlation with the crystallized intelligence factor, though it differs very little from the correlation with the fluid intelligence factor. Thus such subjects as mathematics, grammatical analysis, classical languages, and physics correlate as highly as .8 with intelligence, while the *g*-saturation of subjects like geography, painting and drawing, and some skilled performances in athletics, correlate very little with intelligence, though they may involve memory and manual dexterity and such like abilities to a greater extent.

It is probable that quite a number of performances in everyday life, in occupations and elsewhere correlate relatively little with intelligence, but the schools have seemingly chosen as their teaching ground the more abstract and intelligence-demanding subjects, presumably because these are matters that are not picked up easily and automatically in everyday life experience.

Recently the question which Spearman raised, of the relative *g*-saturation of school subjects, has come up for discussion in new terms and situations, notably by Jensen, who has referred to "A" and "B" school subject curricula. The first covers those that demand a good deal of intelligence, like mathematics, physics, etc., and the second those that demand little, like finger painting, learning under certain ways of teaching geography and history, and so on. Actually the distinction is quite an old one going back at least to the middle ages where the scholastics recognized two levels of performance in what were called the quadrivium, of arithmetic, astronomy, music, and geometry, and the trivium, which covered three subjects easily learnt, namely, grammar, logic and rhetoric. Thus what some educators like Jensen are calling the "A" curriculum is analogous to the quadrivium and that called the "B" curriculum would play the role of the trivium of medieval times.

In medieval times the distinction was mainly one of sequence, in that one went through the trivium first and the quadrivium afterwards, omitting the latter unless one proposed to go far in clerical education. But the division today was put forward on quite a different ground, namely, that teachers seem to be having great difficulty in teaching the "A" type of subjects to many children who seemed to be puzzled and frustrated by them and reduced to a low sense of self confidence and interest in school work. Jensen was, indeed (1980) openly proposing that the curriculum be made easy in order that more persons might graduate through it. In the recent (April, 1983) report to the President on American education it was substantiated that average performance has been on the decline for at least a decade and that this decline is greatest in science and mathematics. Since the latter are among the most *g*-loaded subjects this fits my data and hypothesis concerning a one point fall of I.Q. within the generation, due to a dysgenic birth rate, especially since the other features I predicted, e.g. the crime rates, are also present (Cattell, 1983b). However, the finding in the Department of Education report that teachers' classroom grades went up while the more precise objective test results went down would suggest the alternative of supplementary hypothesis that permissiveness, associated with a decline in home and school demands on morale, is also responsible.

If one were to adopt the philosophy and the policy of adapting divisions of schools and curricula to the known distribution of intelligence, it would probably result in a threefold rather than a twofold division, since the normal distribution curve can be cut with greater clarity of separation by putting the middle 50% in one group and the top-most 25% in another and the lower 25% in another. The average I.Q. score in the middle group would, of course, be 100, and that of the upper and lower groups would be well distinguished from this at values of about 85 and 115. On the other hand, though occupations are not everything in life, a division slightly different from this might be made on the grounds of the higher level of education to be demanded from different sections of the work force. Thus the whole class of occupations which we call professional, and all of which demand a pretty good intelligence level, might amount only to a seventh or an eighth of the population, while the unskilled work at the lower level which largely demands steady application, might cover as much as 30% of the population. The division of schools into elementary, intermediate, and secondary in Great Britain between 1920 and 1945 approximated this. However, the advance in actual job distributions, toward a higher proportion of clerical and technically skilled occupations, might now dictate a somewhat different array of schools channels.

Instead of tackling the question of intelligence in relation to curriculum by creating different types of schools, some countries have preferred a single school, with varying degrees of reclassification for different subjects. The argument for a single social group in school is that one half then learns how the other half lives, though the counter argument is that progress is impeded in school achievement in the higher intelligence group.

In as much as some primary abilities are little correlated with others, which seems to be the case in artistic performance and in music, as well as athletic performance, there is an argument in the structure of abilities themselves for keeping a single comprehensive school, along with a re-streaming on particular subjects. For example, talent in music is actually rather rare, depending on an ability to judge absolute pitch as well as on sense of rhythm, and since these abilities prove to be little related to intelligence, it makes good sense to reclassify children in, say, high and low teaching groups in such areas, but in quite a different grouping of the children from that in regard to mathematics and physics.

In this connection greater reliability of practical application could be reached by extending psychological tests measurement from intelligence tests to tests in the primary abilities. In practice this is no great problem, since, if an intelligence test takes about an hour, and a primary abilities test about an hour and a half, as in the up-to-date Hakstian test (1978) one is only taking half a morning out of a child's school life to establish reclassifications with better confidence. Incidentally, one would of course repeat this testing once every two years, or even every year, in view of some changes that may take place in the primary ability levels, though, as indicated, the likelihood of a change of more than 5 points on an I.Q. score is not very high. Nevertheless reliable practice demands more routine retesting than has been characteristic. Indeed, one of the chief objections to Sir Cyril Burt's classification of British school children on the basis of intelligence tests was that the tests were taken only once at the age of 11 years when the separate streams developed, whereas good practice would have called for repeating the testing at any rate once a year for the next 3 years and reclassifing borderline children according to the results.

6. The Extent to Which Predictions From Tests Can be Extended to Minority Groups and Special Situations.

Although it can be said that in a fairly uniform population and in the conditions that operate in an essentially well organized society, intelligence tests and other forms of psychological tests have proven themselves very valuable, criticism has developed especially in the 60s regarding the fairness of tests to minority groups. Two purely technical psychological questions are involved here, plus a general question of philosophy in society. The technical questions are: 1) is there evidence that the *structure* of abilities is the same in minority groups as in society generally? and 2) are the *levels* of performance on the various structures, such as fluid and crystallized intelligence, spatial ability, verbal ability, etc. significantly different or equal? The philosophical question we will come to in due course. Contrary to what has often been alleged, the structure of abilities does seem to be very similar, as shown, for example, by Horn and Cattell, Jensen and others. For that matter the structure of abilities seems to be very similar even if one goes to foreign countries. For example, the structure of the culture fair intelligence test in Germany comes very close indeed to the same saturations for the various subtests as was obtained in America ((Weiss, 1969) See also Guilford, (1967)). There is also the question of whether intelligence correlates with achievement in much the same way. It would be quite possible that there are differences here, and Lynn's results in Japan (1977) could be partly explained by supposing that school competition is so much more intense in Japan that the correlation of achievement with intelligence becomes higher. However, Humphreys, who has entered into the debate on the fairness of the intelligence tests to blacks in America, shows that the correlation of intelligence with school performance is very similar within a black group to that within a white group (Stanley, 1971). In general, both within social status groups and across countries, therefore, the main conclusion would be that the structure of abilities is very similar, e.g., there is fluid and crystallized intelligence in different countries and there are primary abilities that take much the same form. Further, the mode of operation of these abilities in producing achievement seems to be not very different in the sense that the correlations are not radically of a different order between, say, achievement and intelligence in different groups.

The embarrassing question that remains, therefore, concerns the reality of differences of average ability in different minority groups within the United States, or of different countries. That quite significant differences of average score in ethnic subgroups exist is unquestionable, and it is primarily the *interpretation* of these differences about which debate should seek an answer. Thus in the United States the blacks, the Indians and some other groups score substantially below the white average, while the Jews score above and there is some suggestion that oriental groups also score somewhat above (Lynn, 1977). A thorough examination of this question by an impartial set of scientists is found in the book by Loehlin, Lindzey & Spuhler (1975). The biggest difference so far found is that between blacks in the United States and the white average, which has repeatedly been found to be in the neighborhood of 15 points of I.Q. Difficulties constantly arise in journalistic discussions of findings in the human sciences due to the quite appalling lack of simple statistical education in the high schools. Thus the statement that there is a 15 point difference in average tells us nothing immediately about an *individual,* white or black. It does tell us that there will be considerable overlap of the two groups, such that if we operate on probability we would not get very far in inferring a person's I.Q. from his racial group. It also tells us, however, that if we look for persons with I.Q.s of above, say, 130, which is a cutting point sometimes used for upper professional performances, the chances of finding a black among 1,000 or of a white among 1,000 to exceed 130 is far higher in the second group. That is to say, it is towards the ends of the distributions that the differences in frequency of individuals of the given intelligence level become very noticeable.

Unfortunately, the bulk of the findings Shuey (1958), McGurk (1967), Eysenck (1971), Shockley (1970) of this 15 point difference has been based on traditional intelligence tests. Psychologists have indeed been slow in their technical grasp of the difference between fluid and crystallized intelligence and the differences of inference to be drawn from culture fair, fluid intelligence measures on the one hand and traditional, crystallized intelligence tests on the other. Wherever we expect a difference to be due largely to culture adequate investigation should obviously have been made with culture fair intelligence tests. As yet such testing is by no means adequate, but it does show as mentioned beforehand, that say Chinese in Taiwan, English in the English elementary schools, or French, German, and U.S. school children all performed much the same on the culture fair intelligence tests. Nevertheless, the indications are generally that where an ethnic group has fallen, say, below the majority average in the United States on a traditional intelligence test it also tends to fall below the average on the culture fair test, though not to the same extent.

Actually, if one looks at primary abilities one again gets some significant differences among ethnic groups, which, again, have to be carefully interpreted in terms of possible causes. Figure 4 shows some results along this line.

As suggested above it is important to keep in mind throughout this section that statistically significant differences of means are consistent with considerable overlap among the groups and therefore do not justify any inference about an individual's intelligence on the basis of his group affiliation. On the other hand unless we understand the existence of these differences we may draw some very false conclusions from evidence on the percentages of different ethnic groups in, say, different occupations. The fact is that we should expect fewer persons in a professional occupation demanding substantial intelligence from a group that falls below the general average, and more persons, from one above. For example, in the U.S. there are relatively more Jewish persons in advanced physics, the law, and similar high intelligence professions, reflecting at least in part the mean group difference of that group from others.

As stated above, an up-to-date general survey of ethnic group differences is available in Loehlin, Lindzey & Spuhler, but the psychologist who has met the issue of ethnic and racial differences head on, and has handled a hot potato which few psychologists were prepared to touch, has been Arthur Jensen, in three well known books (1972, 1973, 1980). Eysenck in Britain has also written with technical skill on these issues (1971).

On the question of how much of these differences is inherent and genetic versus cultural, there are wide differences of opinion, with writers like Jensen and Eysenck on one side and Kamin (1974), Lewontin (1970) and Vernon (1982) on the other. In speaking of the use of psychological tests in the schools the question of heritability of intelligence cannot be dodged. It is, however, a very complex subject and can scarcely be handled here except in the briefest of outlines. There are two main methods of investigating behavior genetics, i.e., mental inheritance, namely, the *twin method* and the *multiple abstract variance analysis (MAVA) method.* In the twin method one compares the differences of identical twins on a trait measure with the differences of fraternal twins. If the difference of the former is much less then we can say that there is

Figure 4

Differing Racio-Cultural Primary Ability
(Possibly Crystallized Intelligence) Patterns

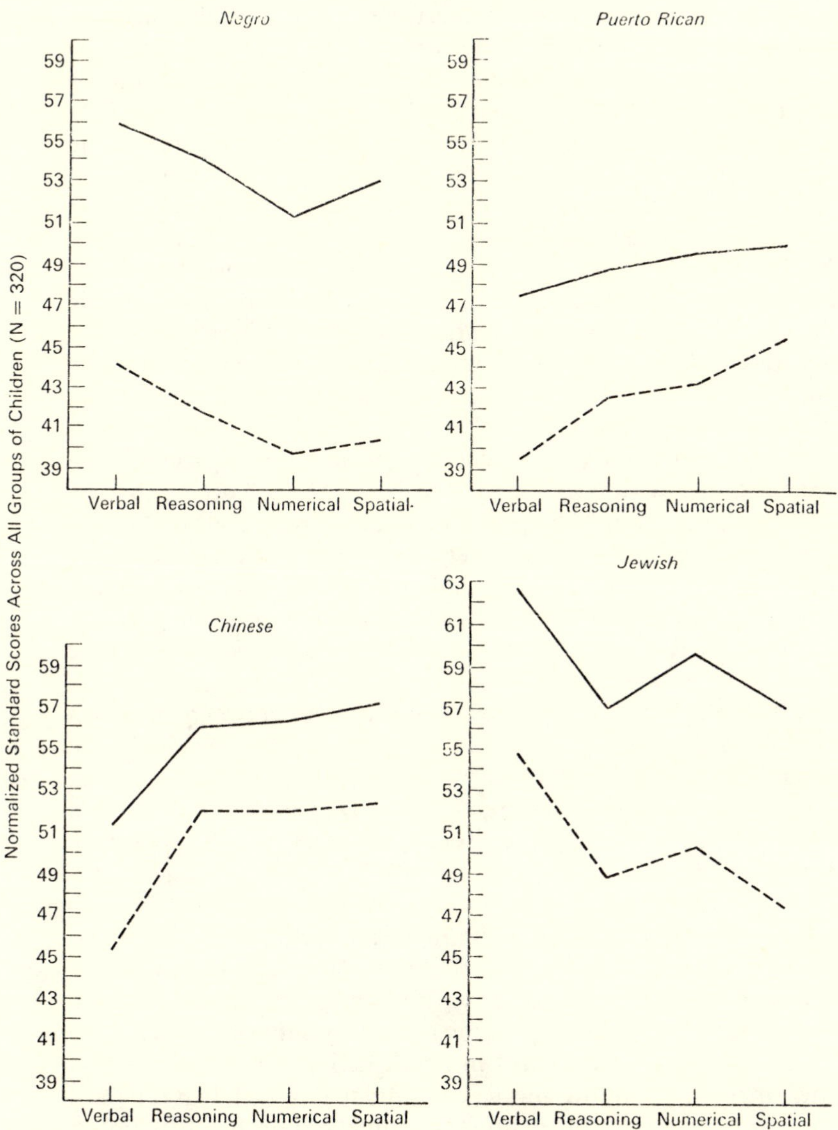

From "Mental abilities of children from different social class and cultural groups," by Lesser, G.S., Fifer, G. and Clark, D. H. Monographs of the Society for Research in Child Development, 1965, 30, #4 (series number 102). © 1965 by the Society for Research in Child Development, Inc.

substantial heredity in the trait, since the fraternal twins differ genetically just as any pair of sibs would. The MAVA method, which the present writer introduced some years ago, is more complex, involving comparisons of unrelated children reared together, of true sibs reared apart, and several other constellations. Briefly, the conclusion as of 1982 seems to be that the variance of intelligence in our present population is, in terms of crystallized intelligence, about 50/50, but nearer to 70% or 80% inherited in the case of fluid intelligence. It is part of the complexity of the issue that this figure will differ according to whether we are talking about variance within the family or variance between families and also that it will vary somewhat in different societies. There is also the question of whether environmental forces act in cooperation with the genetic differences or oppose them. That is to say, is there positive or negative correlation between the impinging environmental influence and the genetic deviation of the individual from the mean? Opinion in the general public, and also in psychologists who have not been very much engaged in research, seems to be an expectation of a positive correlation, i.e., "unto him that hath shall be given." The present results do not support this and point to a quite significant negative correlation. This is tentatively interpreted today as meaning that in the classroom situation in comprehensive schools teaching tends to bring pressure more strongly upon the less intelligent and to keep the more intelligent marking time.

The whole matter of expected differences between groups in regard to school performance, as inferred from psychological tests, has been thoroughly surveyed by Jensen in over the past two decades *Educability and Group Differences* (1973) and there is also much data in Jencks *Inequality* (1972) and in Eysenck's *The Inequality of Man* (1973). Eysenck's *Race, Intelligence, and Education* (1971) also takes up this question with regard to the West Indian immigration into English schools, concluding that significant differences do exist though not of the magnitude of those found with the black group in the U.S.

The fact that most researchers discover substantial heritability for intelligence does not in itself justify the conclusion that the differences found between ethnic and racial groups are genetic in nature. It does however, suggest a probability, unless other evidence points against this. In the course of the last twenty years there have been several studies claiming to produce substantial changes in I.Q. in children from underprivileged homes, and this of course has been the basis of "Headstart" and similar programs. There is a considerable discrepancy between the report of these studies in the press and the report of them in scientific papers after they have been edited by competent researchers. In a brief survey of such studies by a very eminent educational psychologist, David Glass (1968), aptly named "Piltdown man in Education," the general conclusion he has drawn is that on a first newspaper report a 20 point gain in I.Q. is reported. In a report at a scientific meeting, where more critical standards have to be adopted, it falls to about a 10 point increment. After the results have been combed for false statistical procedures by competent analysts it is likely to fall to about 2 or 3 points (Page, 1940)! There would naturally be no improbability in improvements being brought about in tests of crystallized intelligence, both through the effect of repeated testing in what Vernon calls "test sophistication" and also because the individual becomes acquainted with specific learnt discriminations in a particular field. But that gain is gradually lost as the specific intensive training in the given field is discontinued and in any case it does not seem to spread to other fields, either other fields of crystallized intelligence expression, or in fluid intelligence measures, as Feingold, Sarason and the present writer have shown (1941). We shall return to a broader discussion of the implication of these group differences in Section 8, after discussion of related matters in Section 7.

7. The Extent to Which Prediction of Achievement, Scholarship Selection and Vocational Counseling Can be Improved by Adding Personality and Motivation Tests to Ability Tests

The main theme here is the use of intelligence and other ability tests in education. But it would be a mistake to consider ability tests in isolation, because their full predictive possibilities cannot be understood by sound psychological theory unless we also include personality and motivation measures. Moreover, although up to this point most educational psychologists have stayed with ability tests, it is inevitable that in the future their technical skills will move on to the use of a combination of ability and personality tests.

To prepare for discussion in this section a very brief digression must be made into personality and motivation tests. It has taken about half a century to reach the same level of clarity in regard to personality structure as was achieved by Spearman and Thurstone in the first 30 years of this century in the field of abilities. What we recognize now in the personality field is that no matter whether one approaches by ratings of behavior in everyday life or by questionnaires, or by situational performance test of personality, one arrives at roughly some 20 primary factors and some 8 or 9 secondary (second order) factors. It is still not always clear what the origins of these separate structures are. Among the primaries we recognize proof of Freud's notion of an ego structure and a super ego structure, of Bleuler's conception of a schizothyme and cyclothyme temperament dimension, of Jung's notions of extroversion and introversion, as well as some half dozen factors which could not be perceived at the clinical level but required the microscope of multivariate, factor analytic methods. The same structures have been shown to exist at different age levels, developing through childhood, and also in different cultures, in that structure of the *16 Personality Factor Questionnaire*, the *Clinical Analysis Questionnaire*, and the *High School Personality Questionnaire* all seem to be much the same in Anglo-Saxon countries, in France, Italy, Germany, Japan, etc. We can thus conclude that we are dealing with essentially universal dimensions of human nature. Furthermore, we can give scores to these from questionnaires and from the OA batteries (Cattell & Schuerger, 1978) which permit a profile to be set up for any given individual across some 16 to 28 factors.

The development of objective motivation strength factors, i.e., measures of the strength of interests by other than questionnaires, which are fallible in measuring motives, is the latest development of all. Such tests as the *Motivational Analysis Test* and the *School Motivational Analysis Test* are now yielding criteria on relationships in education and in clinical psychology. These motivation tests measure dynamic structures about half of which are the primary drives, as found in the primates and the mammals generally, and another half of them are acquired patterns representing learning from such institutions as the church, the family, the peer group, the occupation, recreation area, and so on.

As soon as these new measures became available Cattell & Butcher (1958), with a substantial grant from the Office of

Education, set out to investigate how much prediction of school achievement could be obtained from these measures in conjunction with intelligence tests. Their book, *The Prediction of Achievement and Creativity*, came out in 1968 and immediately vindicated the common observation of teachers that personality and character qualities could be as important as abilities in predicting school achievement. As with the primary abilities, there were differences in *the combinations of traits* that predicted this and that area of school achievement, but there were also some very broad results common to virtually all fields of grade prediction. Thus it was found that the super ego strength, as one might well expect, is positively predictive of school achievement, over and above intelligence, that self sufficiency is also important, and that assertiveness and pugnacity are negatively related, as also is surgency. What is called the specification equation assigns weights to each of these 16 personality factors in the prediction of general achievement as follows: (Cattell & Butcher, 1968)..

$$Ach = .15A + .50B + .10C... + .25G... + .20Q_2 + .20Q_3$$

Only the more loaded and better known personality traits are included here, A being cyclothyme tendency, B intelligence, C ego strength, G super ego strength, Q_2 self sufficiency and Q_3 the self sentiment. It is important to notice that although some of the names might suggest identity, the measurements by the *Motivation Analysis Test* are what is called "in new factor space," beyond that of the personality factors. That is to say, they definitely add information which is not present in the above *general* personality factor measures. The finding from the motivation area can be summarized by Figure 5 which shows the factors which distinguish the overachiever from the underachiever in the dynamic field. It will be seen that the super ego and the self sentiment are powerful contributors, and that pugnacity and gregariousness contribute negatively. In some ages the strength of the sex drive is also contributing negatively.

The result of this pioneer survey of the contributions of the three domains of psychological tests can be summarized in Table 2.

What this table indicates is that with these high school students ·the I.Q. continues to contribute what it has hitherto typically been found to do, namely, a correlation of plus .5 and a contribution to the variance, therefore, of 25%. The combined personality factors also contribute about another

TABLE 2

Degrees of Prediction of School Reached by Addition of Personality (HSPQ) & Motivation (SMAT) Traits to Intelligence in High School Children

Test of personality, motivation, and ability	Number of predictor variables	Criteria	
		Standardized achievement test	Average of school grades
SMAT	15	.522 (.282)	.482 (.164)
*HSPQ (less factor B)†	13	.520 (.329)	.597 (.462)
HSPQ + SMAT	28	.688 (.367)	.717 (.449)
HSPQ + SMAT + IQ	29	.854 (.734)	.813 (.650)

Source: Cattell and Butcher (1968).
* HSPQ = High School Personality Questionnaire.
† Factor **B** is a measure of intelligence.
Figures in parentheses are the multiple correlation coefficients corrected for shrinkage.

FIGURE 5

Motivation Traits that Contribute to Over versus Under Achievement (Intelligence Constant)

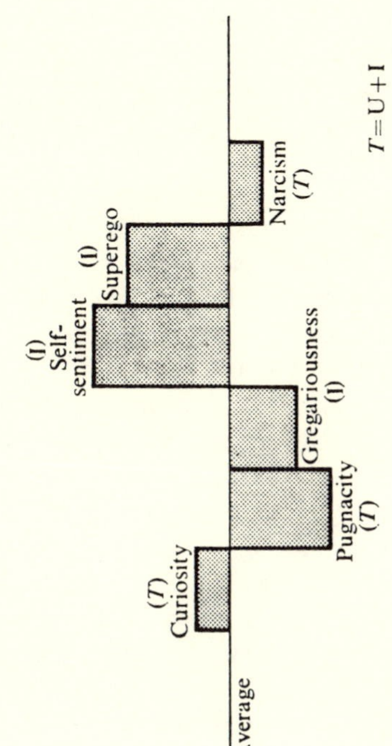

25% of the variance, and the motivation measures contribute close to 20%. Considering that the objective motivation measures here were in their infancy, we might expect that in the future about one quarter of the variance of achievement comes from abilities, one quarter from the general personality traits, and one quarter from motivation. What this means in terms of the learning process is discussed in Cattell 1971, 1980, Gagne 1967, and others.

The statistician will recognize that this is a truly remarkable degree of prediction, since it leaves only 25% to chance, which in these circumstances might be called the home environment, the social class, and other things. Of course, the personality of the child already includes to some extent the consequences of these environmental conditions, so we do not have a clean split of contribution from what is in the individual from contribution that is also the environment. Nevertheless, it shows that the power of psychological tests today to predict school achievement is very great if the psychologist works intelligently with personality and interest measures as well as ability measures.

Among the swings of interest that have taken place in education, that from straight *school performance* to *creativity,* which occupied much attention in the 60s, deserves comment here. The psychological analysis shows pretty clearly that the difference between achievement in regular grades and creativity resides in the personality factors rather than in the ability factors. High intelligence, or high performance on the appropriate primary ability are, of course, *necessary* for creativity. But they do not confer creativity in themselves, and indeed there is some opposition between the personality characteristics that aid achievement in examinations and those which favor creativity. One such is introversion, which is positively connected with creativity, whereas the teacher's idea of the normal child is often an extrovert. A second difference is that dominance (E factor on the High School Personality questionnaire) which favors creativity is negatively related to achievement grades. That is to say, docility, the opposite of the self assertive erg E in the SMAT, favors receptivity to learning and total performance on grade scores. It is interesting that Cattell and his coworkers have shown (1963) that the pattern of the creative personality is almost identical across different fields, e.g., in science, in writing fiction, in art, etc. and that introversion with dominance is the common characteristic.

During the period of increasing emphasis on scholarship selection in England, by means of intelligence tests rather than literal classroom performance, the observation was sometimes made that intelligence tests might reliably be selecting the intelligent child, but that his performance later in life sometimes showed very little more than passive intelligence and a capacity to score in academic examinations. It is certainly very easy to point to examples from, say, William Pitt to Winston Churchill, where school performance had little predictive power in relation to achievements in later life, and it is biographically evident that in these cases the personality factors we have found above were in fact operative. If scholarships, for example, are to be given in anticipation of contributions to society in adult life, rather than examination passing in schools, there is a strong argument for including personality and motivation measures along with ability measures in psychological testing in schools for scholarship purposes.

8. Inherent Test Properties Affecting an Acceptable Use of Psychological Tests in the School System

In this section we have to cover a somewhat miscellaneous set of topics that have to do with the use of psychological tests in schools. These require attention to the degree of technical adaptability and reliability on tests themselves, while in the next section we must deal with broader questions of social situational reaction to testing and turn later to the less condensable social issues. In considering use of tests across the school age range we must note the technical fact that the reliability and validity of intelligence tests is higher at later ages than at earlier ages. There are several reasons for this. First is the obvious one that a child of 6, 7, and 8 cannot be expected to train his concentration upon a problem as readily as can one of 15, 16, or 17, so that some unreliability arises from motivational fluctuations. Secondly our predictions are more blind at this age because we do not know as much about the structure of abilities in really young children as we do at later ages. In consequences, the intelligence tests available are not as reliably interpretable as at later states of development. Indeed, when one gets down to 3 or 4 years of age the evidence seems to be that sheer motor performance is as important in the score on certain tests such as the Merrill Palmer (See Cattell & Bristol,

1933) and the Gesell (1980) measures as what we recognize to be the general factors of fluid and crystallized ability. However, Cattell has shown (1963, 1971) that at least the fluid and crystallized general factors *can* be distinguished in the 4 to 8 year range. In connection with the confounding with manipulative motor skills it is noteworthy that the young chimpanzee at the same age as the human infant is actually ahead in most manipulative skills. However, there are few situations, as far as the school is concerned, where any weight has to be put upon tests before the age of 6, 7, or 8 years. As a consequence of what has just been indicated, particularly the fact that individual testing is essential at the early age, we have decidedly smaller samples on which to base information about distributions of intelligence and differences among groups. In the domain of culture fair intelligence tests, suitable for measuring fluid intelligence, we at least have 3 scales available at successive ages, namely, scale 1 from age 4 to 8, scale 2 from age 8 to 12, and scale 3 above that age into the performance of superior adults (Cattell, 1971).

An important question in regard to the situations in which intelligence tests are given concerns the effect of motivation and rapport with the examiner. There is no doubt that a skilled examiner will get better results through establishing better rapport with the subjects before beginning testing. On the other hand systematic experiments have shown surprisingly little relationship between motivation and test performance (Spearman, 1923, Burt & Williams, 1962). There is considerable relationship between motivation and test performances of a *simple* kind such as speed of tapping or speed of cancellation of letters in the printed page, but relatively little in the more abstract performances. Thus Spearman and others since have arranged to give an intelligence test to a group with minimum motivation and again with some prize such as $5.00 for exceeding one's previous performance, and the result seems to be that the rank order of the subjects remains much the same under the two conditions, though the performance does improve slighly under the stronger motivation. Most well designed intelligence tests put the items in order of increasing difficulty, so that speed does not enter so much into the results, because the more able person proceeds further in any case. Of course, there is ideally the technical trick of correcting for guessing in these selective answer tests. For example, if there are 5 alternative answers a person has a 20% chance of being right even though he has no insight into the problem whatever. These technical aspects of item construction etc. may be studies in books such as Cancro (1971), Cattell (1971) and Jensen (1980).

Another situational circumstance that has to be taken into account in considering intelligence test results is the influence that is called "test sophistication" Adkins (1937), Vernon (1965, 1969). This reflects the gain which takes place in repeated experience of intelligence tests through knowing something about the layout of tests and what to expect in the timing, etc. The fact is that on readministering the same or equivalent tests one finds improvement from the first to the second administration and again between the second and third, gradually diminishing until the point of the fifth or sixth administration when no further improvement takes place. This improvement is not great, corresponding to about 3 to 6 points of I.Q., but there is no doubt that a set of children who have never seen an intelligence test before will not do quite as well as a set of children who have, say, been tested every year on intelligence tests. In the IPAT culture fair intelligence tests there are always 2 equivalent forms, A and B, which are to be given in that order. The norms for B are then slightly different from those for A, allowing for the practice that has occurred on form A. Obviously the alert psychologist will find out if his group has had intelligence tests before and proceed with norms accordingly.

It is usual to give intelligence tests with a time limit for each sub-test which permits only the brightest to complete the test. This is really a concession to practicality since if one gave an intelligence test in the class period without time limits there would naturally be some who would still be working on the test long after the class ends. As Spearman found, the results show that a set of candidates of much the same age come out in much the same order when the test is administered with a time limit and without a time limit, but, of course, the norms must be different in the two cases.

While dealing with time limits one must note that there have been constant pressures from school teachers, but more particularly in industry, for shorter and shorter intelligence tests. In many cases test designers have succumbed to this. One way of succumbing to it is to use only one kind of sub-test as was the case in the Miller analogies or the Raven matrices, but this is unacceptable from the standpoint of knowledge of ability structure. Every sub-test of one type contains a *specific* ability as well as the *general* intelligence it is supposed to measure. Consequently, one tries to reduce the effect of intrusion of a specific ability by having, say, 6 or more different sub-tests all of good saturation on the general factor and operating with different specifics. Thus if one wishes to measure fluid intelligence it is better to use the culture fair test with some 4 or more different sub-tests than the Raven matrices, which also aim at fluid intelligence, but rest on only one type of sub-test.

We have already discussed above the social aspects of intelligence testing that has to do with problems of difference of performance among different ethnic groups. As there stated a good deal of this difference persists even with a switch to culture fair intelligence tests. There are also social status differences in performance which have evoked much debate. Typically the intelligence level of people in different occupations will be significantly different and in as much as inheritance of intelligence occurs there will be differences in children's scores according to the social status, occupationally, of their parents. With ordinary intelligence tests which measure crystallized intelligence this correlation between intelligence of the child and occupational and educational level of the parent has been about the magnitude of .3 (McArthur & Elley, 1963). This is quite a small correlation and accounts for only one tenth of the variance, since the fraction of variance accounted for is the square of the correlation coefficient. This low value is understandable in view of the fact that chance plays its role everywhere in occupational success, and also in terms of the wide standard deviation of intelligence which we know exists in any one occupation. If culture fair intelligence tests are used the correlation falls from about .3 to .2 indicating, as would be expected, that part of the superior performance of children of higher social status arises from the educational background advantages in their families. If one is thinking in terms of recruitment of resources in high intelligence, say above an I.Q. of 130, then a higher proportion of children of I.Q. 130 and above will be found in professional families than in skilled workers and a higher proportion in skilled workers than in unskilled workers. However, due to the relatively large proportion of the population in the last category, it turns out that the *absolute* number contributed is still greater from the lower strata than from the upper strata (Cattell, 1938). This statistical consideration which justified the educational plan which Sir Cyril Burt introduced in England of selection according to intelligence tests rather than immediate school achievement, and which resulted in such a remarkable transformation in the proportion of students with working class parents in the ancient universities of Oxford and Cambridge, for example, justifies more use of intelligence tests in the educational system.

The notion that whole groups – be they cultural groups, racial groups, or regional groups – may differ significantly in intelligence (even on culture fair tests, which suggest one is dealing with a genetic difference) is one that is accepted with difficulty by most journalists and probably the general public. The fact is that urban groups generally score higher on intelligence than rural groups, and that various migratory selections produce average differences of I.Q. Thus Lynn, dividing Great Britain into a number of regions, shows that intelligence test results from the schools show significant differences according to region and that other features of the region are related to these intelligence differences. For example, the proportion of students who go to the university, the inverse of the infantile death rate, the average real earnings, etc. relate themselves to the average intelligence level. It is of course, debatable which is cause and which is effect, but if we are dealing with reasonably culture fair intelligence tests the suggestion is that some migratory tendencies have persisted over many generations in Britain and produced some real differences of mean between the regions. Something approaching this has been demonstrated by Thorndike and Woodyard (1942) in America, in as much as different cities showed a tendency to statistically different score levels. One would surely expect that a region of attractive climate and other conditions such as, say, Santa Barbara in California, would attract more intelligence than a city, say, such as Detroit, and that this would occur simply through a process of voluntary selection going on for many years. In general there is nothing much one has to do about this, since the aim of testing is to treat each individual on his own merits. However, one needs to take even comparatively small differences in mean into account in *understanding* why there are differences from different regions. For example it is quite unfair to accuse teachers of responsibility for poor performance in a region where the performance of the children is poorer than another, since this may be partly or largely due to the differences in distribution of child intelligence in the two places. Furthermore it is well recognized that the rate of progress of children in a particular classroom is determined quite as much by the level of the child's associates as by the quality of the teaching. The prediction of achievement from intelligence therefore has to take into account the ambient situation in the classrooms, in that a child of, say, I.Q. 100 in a class averaging I.Q. 95 will not make such progress as a child of I.Q. 100 in a class averaging 105. Extensions of discussion of questions of this kind will be found in Jensen's *Educability and Group Differences* (1973). It will be recognized from this that the final best prediction of scholastic performance from tests requires not only the use of general intelligence tests and primary ability tests, along with personality and motivation measures, but also an allowance for the teaching circumstances, in which the type of class companionship is important. There are often not easily defined but persistent cultural atmospheres to be taken into account in this connection. For example in Hawaii, the Hawaiian culture is unsympathetic to individual competition whereas in, say, New York, individual ambition is approved and the child is accustomed to commendation from his parents and others for higher achievement in a competitive situation. Among native Hawaiians it is more usual for the solidarity of the group to show up in disapproval of the individual who tries to show he knows more than his peers. Of course, this latter, as a peer culture, is not lacking as a motive, say, in English public schools, where a "swot" who studies hard is sometimes looked at askance as having gone over too much to the values of his teachers, but it is by no means as pervasive and complete in its effect on motivation as in, say, a native Hawaiian group.

9. Social Reactions to Psychological Testing

Before looking at what the present state of the art of psychological assessment suggests in terms of school testing installations, let us look at what the problems are in regard to social readiness to permit the advances in psychology as a science to be applied to the school system.

Between 1945 and 1975 a revolt occurred in some circles against examinations in general and intelligence testing in particular, which has actually reached the point of creating legislation in some states against the use of intelligence tests. The causes of this deserve examination, if we are to understand what to do, but they are complex causes that would need much more space than we have here for their substantiation. Probably two different origins are mainly to be considered. First after Sputnik went up in 1957 there was such a shock to the conviction of American technical superiority that there was a call for increased pressure in the schools for achievement, particularly in the sciences. This call for pressure seems to have evoked a counter-culture, appearing under various manifestations and names such as the "beatnik" culture, the "me" generation and so on. In student revolts in the universities in the 60s it took the form of objection to examinations and the view that the avant-garde position on testing was that the individual should only be compared with his own previous performances and not with the performances of others. It resembled the view in Omar Khayyam about the day of judgement:

> They talk of some strict Testing of us – Pish!
> He's a Good Fellow and 'twill all be well.

The second source, and it was one with sharper political edges, came from the minority groups, principally the blacks, who showed up with poor performance both on the intelligence tests and on the standardized schools performance examinations. The view was that the tests were in some way biased against minorities and new intelligence tests were invented to handle this. The upshot, briefly, was that this did not alter the main effect and that one had in the end to recognize that there was likely to be a steady and persistent difference in mean performance from different ethnic groups.

The revolt had origins from a far wider field than response to testing itself so far as a brief summary of the above can venture to conclude. It sprang from 1) the post-war movement toward general permissiveness in the narcissistic "me" generation, 2) the questioning of authority due to the Viet Nam War, 3) the discontent of minorities with the findings on tests, 4) notably in Britain, a left-wing condemnation of "elites", and 5) perhaps the reaction in American schools to the above "Sputnik" pressure.

Back of 1) and 4) particularly has been a simple-minded misunderstanding of the words, due largely to Jefferson and Franklin, that "all men are created equal." These authors obviously never for a moment believed in biological equality, but only in that equality of rights and opportunities, along with abolition of unfair privilege and the inauguration of promotion by talents, for which both the French and American revolutions had fought. Although equal opportunity and a culture aimed at a meritocracy have a minor distinction (in that the latter adds that the more able should also govern) they necessarily involve similar procedures. And here we meet a psychological force that has always existed, apart from the events of 1965 to 1975, namely an envy of superior performance. This is well studied by Nathaniel Weyl (1969) in his analysis of the role of envy in historical situations, associated with destruction of leaders. Herrnstein (1973) also recognizes this in his book on *I.Q. and the Meritocracy* and Young in *The Rise of the Meritocracy* (1958). In short, human nature is such that, even if one works to do away with privilege, individual differences will not be eliminate. See Dixon & Johnson (1980), Osborne, Noble & Weyl (1978), Williams (1956), and Burt (1959). In certain cultures more jealousy than admiration may be directed at superior performance. That is to say, even if we set up fair devices to let the more able and dedicated rise to leadership position it will not destroy the projection of envy against such groups. The matters just discussed deserve being brought more prominently in the mass media into a healing illumination, since the cost of such tendencies is considerable. For example, the aboliton of intelligence testing from school systems has clearly resulted in a recrudescence of misplacement of students in regard to appropriate opportunities. It has led to misunderstandings of causes of backwardness, (associated with unfair pressures being put upon the less able) and in rising costs in industry through having square pegs in round holes. What actually happened in many English schools when the Labour government abolished the "11 plus" intelligence test selection built by Burt and many other progressive psychologists was a return to evaluation by the headmaster, who could not possibly know the capacities of all the children under his charge and who might be subject to pressure from privileged parents. The role of political and general social forces in detail here had better be studied by a historian of education, but from a psychologist's viewpoint the outcome can only be compared to the state of agression in the medieval world that arose out of the ruins of the orderly Roman Empire.

The technical criticisms of intelligence selection – which may well be rationalizations for the more emotional objections discussed above – were on the surface 1) that intelligence was not nearly as much inherited as had been argued and that in fact the constancy of the I.Q. was an artifact on which no basic arguments for school organization should be placed, 2) that testing children only once at 11 years of age did not give reliable evaluation, and 3) that this testing put a great strain on the child because his parents realized that much of his career thereafter depended on his performance then. There is *some* truth in each of these objections, particularly in the notion that an intelligence test and a school achievement test applied just at the end of one particular semester could not be a fair assessment of the child's potential. There could also be objections from a psychologist on the grounds that newer culture fair, intelligence tests were not used, and on the grounds that personality traits, which also have some degree of permanence, and which also predict future achievement, were not taken into account in promotion.

When the greater present day technical reliability of selection is accepted, there still remains a principle to be settled regarding special educational expenditure. Should it be on the top, say, 10% of highly gifted children or on the lagging 10% of dull and backward children? Aware as we presently are of falling standards in literacy etc., both compassion and the need for a dependable electorate call for doing all we can do to lift the level of those in the I.Q. 75 and below range. Appropriate teaching requires there be at least twice the expenditure per child than is given to the normal. But the reliable research evidence is that the results are quite small in reducing illiteracy in the truly lower borderline defective group. A eugenist is compelled to argue that the social conscience should, in terms of family planning have shifted the higher birth rate in the first place from the I.Q. 70-80 range to the I.Q. 120-130 range.

Incidentally, the third cause of opposition to testing – mainly the black minority objection – can be set aside as far as fact and logic are concerned, for with suitable tests there is no evidence of poor performance being associated with ethnic minorities as such. As mentioned above the Jewish and the Chinese minorities actually tend to perform above the general American average.

Meanwhile all that is labelled as concern about the "exceptional child" continues to ignore the exceptionally bright and *their* needs. There is sufficient evidence, e.g., in the negative correlation of environmental stimulation and innate intelligence level (Cattell, 1982) to justify the conclusion that what little "streaming" of brighter and duller classes is now accepted fails to save the bright from boredom and from performance below their true potential. Yet these are the people on whom the safety and prosperity level of the nation will especially depend.

The principle that longer and more challenging education should be given to the innately better endowed gets questioned mainly through lack of understanding of human ability structure. The same people that question this in regard to intelligence will recognize that when a child is so tone deaf that he cannot distinguished the national anthem from Pop Goes the Weasel you do not waste prolonged musical education on him – incidentally at the cost of his own exasperation.

Education addresses itself partly to establishing the general educational foundations necessary for occupations, and partly to developing full expression of the individual in cultural, political and other fields. The latter is hard to focus, quantitatively by present concepts and methods, but the problem in occupations is relatively clear, namely, that we have a shortage of people available for the occupations needing higher intelligence and education, while we seem to have an excess of persons who are able only to handle unskilled work. Unfortunately for this state of affairs, the whole trend in this century has been towards creating more complex, intelligence-demanding occupations. Thus as the present writer has shown in more detail elsewhere (1982) a dislocation has occurred between the distribution of demands, and, on the other hand, the distribution of the supply of abilities. The abilities, of course, reach levels determined by training superimposed on inherent intelligence, but the latter, alone, can produce, by the wrong kind of birth rates, a dislocation. The dislocation between the curves of supply and demand inevitably lead to unemployment in the less skilled occupations and a perhaps excessive earning differential in the market value of the highly able and creative individuals (1982).

The losses in cultural productivity through this neglect of the selected bright are, of course, difficult to document, as is any creativity. (See however, Cattell & Brennan's (1982) relation of national I.Q. to national productivity). What brings the relation home to those who think more at the basic level of national security is such examples as I cite elsewhere about performance in war. In the highly technical warfare of today the alarm about the higher production of qualified scientists by the Soviets relative to the U.S.A. is fully justified.

This has been discussed on TV, for example, in terms of supply of teachers, but it also has to do with the supply of exceptionally bright students. And to be realistic this must be considered also a eugenic problem. Perhaps because teachers have been inclined to align with nurture in nature-nurture controversies, they have been slow to turn their attention to the sources of good quality in the raw material of their trade. Unlike builders who protest at having to make bricks from straw they tend to look no further than at what they are given. They seem to have been afraid to get involved in eugenic issues, yet the supply of intelligent children is really their problem more than that of any other institutional group. It is very probable that an unbiased educational psychological survey would show as suggested above that the slight falls in the last decade in certain educational levels of school reading are partly associated with birth rates.

One wonders where the log-jams are in public thought and policy on these issues. It would be interesting to get a poll to find out what percentage of the general public today misinterprets the statement that "all men are created equal," in the manner discussed above, and how this affects the required broader approach to today's problem of scholastic levels and expenditures. And does the apparent oppposition to acceptance of partly innate difference on psychological tests reside in teachers, parent-teachers associations, or educational administrators? The education of the present adult generation seems sometimes to have been left largely in the hands of journalists and the media, and there can be no doubt that over the last thirty years these verbally facile, scientifically largely untrained "thinkers" have been partly responsible for the present problem. Of the dozens of public-issue-discussing "round tables" on TV I have yet to see *one* that considered eugenic questions or included any leading psychometrist among the politicians, bureaucrats and journalists. The British Broadcasting Corporation, with its talks by Eysenck and other psychologists, and its airing of the Sir Cyril Burt debate, is an encouraging exception to this stifling conspiracy of silence. A fascinating, almost incredible documentation of the situation in American journalism recently appeared in Professor Herrnstein's article concerning major newspapers and the heredity question in the *Atlantic Monthly,* August, 1982, entitled "I.Q. testing & the media." Anyone concerned to understand the origins of the present unintelligent utilization of intelligence tests must first read this, if he is to shape a practicable strategy of public enlightenment.

10. A Plan for the Best "Test Installation" for Developmental Monitoring in Schools at the Present State of the Art of Psychological Testing

As indicated in the introduction, the use of psychological tests in schools has been sporadic, uneven, fluctuating from decade to decade, and confined often to rather special areas. Thus since Binet at the beginning of the century and the various developments by psychologists of measures for the backward child, there has been a pretty consistent use of intelligence tests by school psychologists and psychiatrists and Child Guidance Clinics, to diagnose the causes of backwardness and to direct retarded children into special classes for the retarded. But elsewhere the uses have been sporadic and fugitive.

One of the major losses through absence of a reasonable approach to the problem as indicated in an introductory way above, is, the neglect of the more gifted children in our present educational system. Protests have, it is true, arisen in the last decade to the effect that we have meant by attention to "exceptional children" only concentration on the exceptionally backward and that no administrative category exists for special handling of the exceptionally talented. There is no question that the child of I.Q. 130 or above, such as Terman (1926) studied, loses some of his keeness and suffers some maladjustment in being tied to the pace of the *average* classroom. There have always been, of course, stories that the intellectually bright are in some way emotionally maladjusted, schizophrenic or whatever. This was shown to be a myth first by the extensive studies of Terman who found that, if anything, the children in the high I.Q. category were better emotionally adjusted, of better physical status, and in general above average in other respects than intelligence alone. We have to blame Dryden for putting the popular myth in the couplet:

Great wits are sure to madness near allied,
And thin partitions do their bounds divide

It may well be that in certain ages and situations the more

intelligent have in time become maladjusted, but at least at the age investigated by psychologists today there is, if anything, a moderate positive correlation between intelligence and other desirable personality qualities.

The suggestion here for improving education of the bright in the educational system namely, by having special classes for the exceptionally intelligent, say, 5% of the population, needs to be considered not only from the standpoint of the development of the individual but also of the needs of society. The needs of society in terms of its general cultural standards are obvious but not easy to ducument. Only by turning to a rather brutal issue, namely, that of national security in war, can one pointedly bring out the importance of this talented group. The present writer has referred (1937), for example, to the fact that the performance of individual German U-boat captains differed enormously (in terms of tonnage sunk) and that a few able commanders accounted for far more than all other officers and crews together. Unfortunately destructive acts seem more easily countable than constructive ones, but there is surely little doubt that in what Churchill called "the Wizard War" victory and security is going to depend enormously upon a small percentage of very top brains involved in defense. Here is a very practical reason why we cannot afford to let our most gifted section of the school population be held back by some doctrinaire view that all must march at the same rate and in the same manner through the school system. Likewise it would be true, though less concretely demonstrable, that the losses in national cultural productivity through lack of adjustment of education to talent are just as disastrous.

The rational remedy for the *real* weaknesses brought out by the criticisms to which the Burtian system became subject was to improve the testing not to abolish it. As regards the stress on the child, spreading out the talent evaluation over years would tend to reduce that. It might also be said that the child's future life is going to be full of stresses and that it is part of growing up to learn how to manage them. The question of how much pressure societies put upon children is, of course, an important one and we know that in, for example, both Germany and Japan these competitive stresses are very great, whereas in Britain and America they appear to be less so. This is a matter of national culture which is beyond our analysis or remedying in the present discussion. What we can call for is a more efficient and reliable psychological testing system which might be called a *monitoring* rather than a single decision process. By monitoring we mean that the best possible test installation, i.e., a set of suitable well-standardized intelligence and personality tests, would be incorporated in the regular school procedures in such a way as to occur, say, at yearly intervals from school entry onward. These records could be filed, and, being on a similar system, would be useful when a child moves from one school district to another. They would especially permit more attention to the *process* of development of the child, since there would be records permitting comparisons over times and circumstances. One can think of many cases of adult problems in crime and in mental hospital incarceration where some records of earlier development would have been very valuable indeed in avoiding the final unfortunate outcomes. In short, a consideration of this problem leads one to the conclusion that a simple installation of measurement at yearly or two yearly intervals, based largely on group testing, and requiring very little addition to school organization, could be extremely valuable.

The work upon which this publication is based was performed pursuant to the Contract No. NIE-P-82-0089 of the National Institute of Education. It does not, however, necessarily reflect the views of that agency.

REFERENCES

Adkins, D.C.
1937 The effect of practice on intelligence test scores, *Journal of Educational Psychology*, 28, 222-231.

Binet, A. and Simon
1905 Methodes nouvelles pour le diagnostique du niveau intellectuelle des anormaux, *L'Année Psychologique*, 11, 191-244.

Burt, C.L.
1917 Distribution & Relations of Educational Abilities, London, P.S. King.
1925 The Young Delinquent, London, University of London Press.
1937 The Backward Child, London, University of London Press.
1940 Factors of the Mind, London, University of London Press.
1959 Class differences in general intelligence III, *British Journal of Statistical Psychology*, 12, 15-33.
1961 The gifted child, *British Journal of Statistical Psychology*, 14, 123-139.

Burt, C.L. and E.L. Williams
1962 The influence of motivation on the results of intelligence tests, *British Journal of Statistical Psychology*, 15, 127-136.

Cancro, R.
1971 Intelligence: Genetic and Environmental Influences, New York, Grune and Stratton.

Cattell, J., M. McKeen, R.C. Tarroad and C. Wissler
1901 The correlation of mental and physical tests, *Psychological Review Monographs*, 3, 1-45.

Cattell, R.B.
1934 Occupational norms of intelligence and the standardization of an adult intelligence test, *British Journal of Psychology*, 25, 1-28.
1937 The fight for our national intelligence, London, King.
1938a A study of the national reserves of intelligence, Human Factor, 12, 127-136.
1938b Some changes in social life in a community with a falling intelligence quotient, *British Journal of Psychology*, 28, 430-450.
1943 The measurement of adult intelligence, *Psychological Bulletin*, 40, 153-193.
1963a The personality and motivation of the researcher from measurements of contemporaries and from biography. In C.W. Taylor and F. Barron (Eds), The Identification of Creative Scientific Talent, New York, Wiley.
1963b The theory of fluid and crystallized intelligence; a critical experiment, *Journal of Educational Psychology*, 54, 1-22.
1971 Abilities: Their Structure, Growth and Action, Boston, Houghton Mifflin Company.
1980 Personality & Learning Theory, Vol. 2, New York, Springer.
1982 Inflation and business cycles from the standpoint of psychology, *Journal of Social, Political and Economic Studies*, 10, 36-54.

Cattell, R.B. and H. Bristol
1933 Intelligence tests for mental ages of 4 to 8 years, *British Journal of Educational Psychology*, 3, 142-169.

Cattell, R.B. and J. Butcher
1968 The Prediction of Achievement and Creativity, Indianapolis, Bobs Merrill.

Cattell, R.B., S. Feingold and S. Sarason
1941 A culture fair intelligence test: II Evolution of cultural influence on test performance. *Journal of Educational Psychology*, 32, 81-100.

Cattell, R.B. and R.C. Johnson
1984 Functional Psychological Testing, New York, Brunner-Mazel.

Cattell, R.B. and J.M. Schuerger
1978 Personality Theory in Action. Savoy, Ill.: Institute for Personality & Ability Measurement.

Cohen, J.
1959 The factorial structure of the WISC at ages 7 - 6, 10 - 6 and 13 - 6, *Journal of Consulting Psychology*, 23, 285-299.

Dixon, L.K. and R.C. Johnson
1980 The Roots of Individuality, California Monterey, Brooks Cole Publishing Co.

Eysenck, H.J.
1971 Race, Intelligence and Education, London, Temple Smith.
1973 The Inequality of Man, London, Temple Smith.

Gagne, R.M., ed.
1967 Learning and Individual Differences, Columbus, Ohio, Merrill.

Galton, F.
1883 Inquiries Into Human Faculty and Its Development, London, MacMillan.

Gesell, et al.
1940 The First Five Years of Life: A Guide to the Study of the Preschool Child, New York, Harper.

Glass, J.
1968 Educational piltdown man, *Phi Delta Kappa*, November, 148-151.

Guildford, J.P.
1967 The Nature of Human Intelligence, New York, McGraw Hill.

Hackstian, R. and R.B. Cattell
1978 The Comprehensive Primary Ability Battery (CAB), Illinois, Champaign, IPAT.

Harrell, T.W. and M.S. Harrell
1945 Army General Classification Test scores for civilian occupations, *Educational and Psychological Measurement*, 5, 229-240.

Herrnstein, R.J.
1973 I.Q. in the Meritocracy, Boston, Little Brown & Co.
1982 I.Q. Testing and the Media, *The Atlantic Monthly*, August, 68-74.

Horn, J.L. and R.B. Cattell
1966 Age differences in primary ability factors, *Journal of Gerontology*, 21, 210-220.

Horn , J.L. and R.B. Cattell
1966 Refinement and test of the theory of fluid and crystallized intelligence, *Journal of Educational Psychology*, 57, 251-270.
Jencks, C.
1972 Inequality: A Reassessment of the Effect of Family and Schooling in America, New York, Harper & Rowe.
Jensen, A.R.
1969 How much can we boost I.Q. and scholastic achievement, *Harvard Educational Review*, 39, 1-123.
1972 Genetics and Education, New York, Harper & Rowe.
1973 Educability and Group Differences, New York, Harper & Rowe.
1980 Bias in Mental Testing, New York, MacMillan Free Press.
Kamin, L.
1974 The Science & Politics of I.Q., Potomac, MD, Colbaum.
Lashley, K.S.
1963 Brain Mechanisms and Intelligence, New York, Dover.
Lewontin, R.C.
1970 Further remarks on race and the genetics of intelligence, *Bulletin of the Atomic Scientists*, 26, 23-25.
Loehlin, J.C., G. Lindzey and J.N. Spuhler
1975 Race Differences in Intelligence, San Francisco, Freedman & Co.
Lynn, R.
1977 The intelligence of the Japanese, *Bulletin of the British Psychological Society*, 30, 69-72.
MacArthur, R.T. and W.B. Elley
1963 Reduction of socioeconomic bias in intelligence testing, *British Journal of Educational Psychology*, 33, 107-119.
McGurk, G.C.J.
1967 The culture hypothesis and psychological tests, in R.E. Kutter (Ed) Race and Modern Science, New York, Social Science Press, 367-381.
Osborne, R.T., C.E. Noble and N. Weyl
1978 Human Variation: The Biopsychology of Age, Race and Sex, New York, Academic Press.
Page, J.D.
1940 The effect of nursery school attendance upon subsequent I.Q., *Journal of Psychology*, 10, 221-230.
Pearson, K.
1904 On the laws of inheritance in man II, on the inheritance of mental and moral characters, *Biometrika*, 3, 131-140.
Piaget, J.
1960a The general problem of the psychobiological development of the child, in Tanner, J.N. (ed) Discussions on Child Development Volume 4, New York, International Universities Press.
1960b The Psychology of Intelligence, New Jersey, Patterson, Littlefield, Adams.
Reitan, R.M.
1959 Impairment of abstraction ability in brain damage; quantita-

tive versus qualitative changes, *Journal of Psychology*, 48, 97-102.

Shockley, W.
1970 Cooperative correlation hypothesis for racial differences in earning power, *Proceedings of the National Academy of Sciences*, 66, 245.

Shuey, A.M.
1958 The Testing of Negro Intelligence, Lynchburg, Virginia, Bell Company.

Spearman, C.
1904 General intelligence objectively determined and measured, *American Journal of Psychology*, 15, 201-293.

Stanley, J.C.
1971 Predicting college success of the educationally disadvantaged, *Science*, 171, 640-647.

Stern, W.
1922 Die Intelligenz der Kinder und der Junglichen. Leipzig, Springer, 1922.

Terman, L.M.
1926 Genetic Studies of Genius, Volume 1, London, Harrup & Co.

Thomson, G.H.
1939 The Factorial Analysis of Human Ability, London, University of London Press.

Thorndike, R.L.
1951 Community variables as predictors of intelligence and academic achievement, *Journal of Educational Psychology*, 42, 321-338.

Thorndike, R.L. and E. Woodyard
1942 Differences within and between communities in the intelligence of children, *Journal of Educational Psychology*, 33, 641-656.

Thurstone, L.L.
1938 Primary Mental Abilities, Chicago University Press.

Vernon, P.E.
1965 Ability factors and environmental influences, *American Psychologist*, 20, 723-733.
1969 Intelligence and Cultural Environment, London, Matthewan.
1982 The Abilities and Achievements of Orientals in North America, New York, Academic Press.

Vining, D.R.
1982 On the possibility of a re-emergence of a dysgenic trend with respect to intelligence in American fertility differentials, *Intelligence*, 6, 241-264.

Wechsler, D.
1958 The Measurement and Appraisal of Adult Intelligence, Baltimore, Williams & Wilkins.

Weiss, R.H.
1969 Die Brauchbarkeit des Culture Fair Intelligence Test Skala 3(CFT 3) bei begabungs psychologische Untersuchungen, Diss, Wurzberg.

Weyl, N.
1969 Some comparative performance indexes of American ethnic minorities, *Mankind Quarterly*, 9, 106-128.

Williams, R.J.
1956 Biochemical Individuality, New York, Wiley & Sons.

Young, M.
1958 The Rise of the Meritocracy, London, Thames & Hudson.

TEST SCORES AS MEASURES OF HUMAN CAPITAL AND FORECASTING TOOLS

BARBARA LERNER
Princeton, New Jersey

If we knew what abilities people needed – to develop a modern economy or to maintain one – and could measure those abilities with enough precision to allow for meaningful comparisons between populations, over time and across space, we would have a powerful measure of human capital, and an economic forecasting tool of considerable promise. This essay is an attempt to explore the possibility that we are already in that fortunate position but have not yet seen or exploited our luck because the questions are in one field, and the answers are in another.

Questions about human capital and its impact on the economies of nations are economists' questions, for the most part, and when economists look for measures of human capital, they usually look to traditional measures like "years of schooling completed" or "highest degree received." These measures are linked to the notion of human capital by a set of assumptions: 1) That there is a positive relationship between the abilities needed to run an advanced economy and the things that are taught in schools, and 2) that more time spent sitting in school rooms leads to higher levels of those abilities. These measures are indirect because the abilities themselves are not measured, only other indicators believed to correlate with them. They are also very crude, because the magnitude of the correlation between abilities and indicators is, in each case, an unknown, and an inconstant one at that. Measures with these defects can be and often are seriously misleading but, without more direct and exact measures to compare them with, danger signals may be few and far between. Often, they do not appear at all until long after the optimal time to act – by altering predictions and/or by taking remedial action of some sort – has passed.

Test scores, on the other hand, offer direct measures of a variety of more-or-less specific abilities and, when the tests in question are well-constructed, objective, standardized tests, they are fairly precise measures that can be kept quite constant, over time and across space. Test experts know this; they also know a great deal about at least some of the abilities tests measure best but, because they are usually psychologists or educators and not economists, they tend to be preoccupied with their own non-economic questions, questions about why scores change and about the implications of such changes for individual development and for actions and policies intended to foster it. They do not usually know or care much about economists' questions, and are not likely to notice when the abilities they measure directly are the same as those economists measure indirectly. Economists are not likely to notice either, because they are generally unfamiliar with the range and quality of available psychometric data and of its potential utility.

1. Literacy: Two Measures, Two Forecasts

This is easiest to demonstrate by focusing on literacy and using American data to illustrate the point. Literacy is the obvious example here because its economic relevance is so clear. In advanced industrial economies, it is a necessary requirement for most skilled jobs, manual or nonmanual; in post-industrial economies – computerized service-and-information-oriented ones, for example – it may well turn out to be a requirement for all of them, as suggested by the continuing decline in the number of unskilled jobs available in the United States and in other nations with highly developed economies.(1)

Economists are, of course, aware of these facts and have been studying the impact of literacy on economic development for a long time. In the United States, they usually rely on Census Reports for this purpose because they offer the most complete data available on the American population as a whole, and because they have a wonderful historical sweep – the U.S. Census Bureau has been counting American noses since 1789 and has reported rates of illiteracy in the population since 1870. Initially, they simply asked people if they could read and write or not, and recorded their answers. In 1947, they limited the scope of their inquires by assuming that people with 5 or more years of schooling were, ipso facto, literate; in 1952 they decided that 6 or more years of schooling completed was a safer benchmark for literacy and that, along with self-

(1) U.S. Census Bureau, *Historical Statistics of the United States, Colonial Times to 1970,* Part 1, p. 139 (Washington, D.C.: U.S. Government Printing Office, 1975).

report data on Americans with fewer than 6 years of schooling, has continued to be the criterion, up to the present day. (2)

Using these criteria, the Census Bureau reported that the rate of illiteracy among Americans over the ages of 14 or 15 years was 11.3% at the turn of the century, and declined to 1.2% by 1970. (3) Among Americans aged 14 to 24, the rates reported were lower still, amounting to a mere .6% in 1959 and falling to .2% in 1979. (4) More encouraging still, the long-standing educational gap between white and black Americans seemed to be closing at last, at least in the emerging generation. In 1959, the illiteracy rate for black Americans aged 14 to 24 was only 1.2%, but it was still more than double the white rate; by 1979, the rates were the same for both groups – .2%, according to the Census measures. (5)

On this basis, it would have seemed reasonable – at least to a post hoc noneconomist – to make a number of optimistic forecasts for the U.S. economy in the 1980s, e.g., no shortage of literate workers, no serious structural unemployment problems, and a quick end to the potentially disruptive consequences of black-white disparities in employment and income. Thus far, none of those happy forecasts have been borne out, and familiarity with the results of studies using psychometric measures of the same variable – literacy – suggested that they were not likely to be. Familiarity with these results was not, however, widespread, even among psychometricians, let alone among economists, due, primarily, to the fragmentation of the social sciences and the mutual oblivion that it breeds.

Mutual oblivion and fragmentation nothwithstanding, psychometricians also measured literacy, but only in recent times, and only very intermittently at that, and they added to the confusion by using different tests with different populations at different points in time, each with a somewhat different definition of literacy. (6) The result is a confusing farrago of

(2) Ibid., pp. 364-365.

(3) U.S. Census Bureau, *Statistical Abstract of the United States, 1981,* p. 143.

(4) Ibid., p. 143.

(5) Ibid., p. 143.

(6) Louis Harris & Associates, *Survival Literacy Study,* No. 2036, National Reading Council, September, 1970; Louis Harris and Associates, *The 1971 National Reading Difficulty Index,* New York, 1971 ERIC ED 057 312; Richard T. Murphy, *Adult Functional Reading Study,* Washington, D.C.: National Institute of Education, 1973; N. Northcutt, *Adult Functional Competency: A Summary* (Austin, Texas:

one-shot studies which at first glance seem much less promising than census data. In fact, their potential utility is much greater.

The great strength of these studies is that they contain no built-in assumptions about the relationship between literacy and years of schooling completed or any other variable, for that matter, and they are not subject to the obvious vagaries of self-report data. Psychometricians may not measure literacy often, but they do not need to rely on assumptions when they do, because they measure it directly. They ask people to *demonstrate* their comprehension of simple, written questions by responding appropriately to a fixed number of them in a delimited period of time under controlled conditions.

In 1970, 1971, and 1975, researchers from the National Assessment of Educational Progress (NAEP) did this, using only easy, everyday questions of the sort that are ubiquitous to everyday life and work in a society with an advanced economy.(7) They found that in 1975, the best of the three years studied, 12.6% of all American 17 year olds still enrolled in school were functionally illiterate, unable to respond correctly to even 75% of these easy, everyday items; 44.4% were semi-literate, missing more than 10% but less than 25%. Worst yet, these figures are gross underestimates of the actual extent of illiteracy among American teenagers in the 1970s, because students who dropped out of school at age 16 – approximately 20 to 25% of the total youth population in the last decade or so – were excluded from the NAEP samples. When the necessary additional data on these students are factored in, the over-all rate of illiteracy for cohorts reaching their eighteenth birthday in the 1970s can safely be estimated to have been at least 20%; the semi-literacy rate was probably closer to 60%.(8) And the

University of Texas, March, 1975). *See also* Abraham Carp, "The Reading Problem in the United States," 17, 36-45, in Reginald Corder, *The Information Base for Reading: A Critical View of the Information Base for Current Assumptions Regarding the Status of Instruction and Achievement in Reading in the United States,* Washington, D.C.: Office of Education, 1971; T.G. Sticht, J.S. Caylor, R.P. Kern, and L.C. Fox, "Project REALISTIC: Determination of Adult Functional Literacy Levels," *Reading Research Quarterly,* Vol. 7, 1972, pp. 424-465; Rose-Marie Weber, "Adult Illiteracy in the U.S.," in John B. Carroll & Jeanne Chall (Eds.), *Toward a Literate Society* (New York: McGraw-Hill, 1975).

(7) National Assessment of Educational Progress, *Functional Literacy: Basic Reading Performance* (Denver, Colorado: NAEP, 1976).

(8) Barbara Lerner, *Minimum Competence, Maximum Choice: Second Chance Legislation,* pp. 86-89 (New York: Irvington, 1980a); Barbara Lerner, "The Minimum

black-white gap was still dramatic: 41.6% of all black 17 year olds still enrolled in school in 1975 were functionally illiterate; 82.7% were semi-literate.(9)

On this basis, it would have seemed reasonable to predict serious shortages of literate workers throughout the 1980s and perhaps beyond, along with high levels of structural unemployment, particularly among younger black workers, and increasing difficulty in meeting economic competition from foreign countries with more literate work forces.

2. Higher Abilities: Traditional Measures v. Economic Realities

With regard to questions of international economic competition, it seems clear that human capital alone does not determine outcome. It seems equally clear that it has an impact on it, an impact that cannot be adequately assessed simply by counting – however accurately – the size of each country's literate work force. Something beyond mere literacy – some higher level of knowledge and/or developed abilities, is obviously important too, and must somehow be assessed, if we are to make reasonable comparisons between nations, and reasonable predictions and recommendations based on them.

The Assessment of these higher level abilities is far more difficult than the assessment of literacy because we are much less clear about what they are and because we must, nonetheless, employ a higher level of measurement in assessing them if we are to produce results that have some practical utility. Literacy is not only easier to define, it is also easier to measure because it is a minimum standard, a threshold requirement. There is room for a narrow range of disagreement about exactly where the threshold is, but the basic question posed – how many workers in a country are literate, how many not – is a nominal one, so a simple nominal measure suffices. All that is required is a device that allows us to sort data into two categories, and to count the numbers in each.

Questions about higher abilities, on the other hand, are questions about relative standards, questions about "how much" as

Competence Testing Movement," *American Psychologist,* pp. 1058-1059, Vol. 36, October, 1981a, 1057-1066; Barbara Lerner, "Vouchers for Literacy: Second Chance Legislation," *Phi Delta Kappan,* December, 1981b, 252-255.

(9) Lerner, 1980a, op. cit. at p. 88.

well as about "how many," and there is no fixed reference point for "how much." How much is enough varies; in economic terms, it is a function of the competition that a nation must meet to succeed in a particular market at a particular point in time. To answer questions of that sort, ordinal or equal interval measures are required, measures that allow us to rank order nations according to the respective levels of knowledge and developed abilities attained by their work force, or segments of it, at particular points in time.

When economists try to do this, they generally rely, once again, on the traditional measures of human capital, "years of schooling completed" and/or "diplomas received." This approach does not solve the underlying definitional question – which sorts of higher abilities are important to economic success, which are not – but it does allow us to sidestep the problem by assuming that whatever those unnamed abilities are, they correlate with higher education in a straight forward linear way.

Comparisons between countries based on these assumptions indicate that the United States is far ahead of all potential competitors.(10) In the last two decades, we sent more of our young people to school for longer periods of time than any other nation in the world,(11) and they emerged with more diplomas than any other people on earth. The expansion of education in this country in those two decades was striking, particularly at the college and university level. At the high school level, the great expansion took place earlier, and over a longer period of time. In 1900, less than 10% of all American 18 year olds were high school graduates;(12) in 1950, 56% were. By 1960, that figure had risen to 72.4%, and the percentages remained above the seventy percent mark throughout that decade and the next one, while the actual number of graduates swelled from 1,200,000 in 1950 to more than 3 million by 1980.(13) At the college and university level, enroll-

(10) Barbara Lerner, "American Education: How Are We Doing?" *The Public Interest,* Vol. 69, Fall, 1982, pp. 59-82.

(11) Robert M. Bjork and Stewart E. Fraser, *Population, Education and Children's Futures* (Bloomington, Indiana: Phi Delta Kappa, 1980); Ruth L. Sivard, *World Military and Social Expenditures 1978* (Leesburg, Virginia: WMSE Publications, 1978); U.S. Census, 1981, op. cit., pp. 873-874.

(12) U.S. Census, *Historical Statistics,* op. cit., p. 379.

(13) U.S. Census, 1981, op. cit., p. 157.

ment jumps in the last two decades were manifest in proportional terms as well as in absolute numbers. In 1960, almost a quarter of all U.S. high school graduates between the ages of 18 and 24 were enrolled in college; in 1970, almost a third of them were, and that was true in 1980, too.(14) Freshman enrollment figures were even higher. Throughout the 1970s, approximately half of the members of each American high school graduation group – about a million and a half students a year – went to college.(15)

Available data indicate that no other nation had a comparable educational record, across the board. Towards the end of the twenty year period in question Japan, Russia and Sweden rivalled the United States in the percentages of students graduating from secondary schools but not in the percentages going on to college.(16) Sweden aside, the percentages of secondary school graduates in most western European nations were much lower than they were in America, ranging from 20% to 50% in countries like England, France, Belgium, and Ireland.(17) Percentages in other western European nations were even lower, and more comparable to those in underdeveloped nations. In West Germany, the Netherlands, and Italy, they were below 20%; that was also the case in Iran, Thailand, India, and Chile.(18)

The contrast between the United States and the rest of the world with respect to college admission rates was even greater. No other western nation sent nearly as high a proportion of its secondary graduates on to college; neither did any Communist nation. Until very recently, the Soviet Union seemed to be graduating only about two-thirds of its secondary school students and sending only about 10% of them on to the institutions of higher learning.(19) Work by University of Chicago

(14) Ibid., p. 158.

(15) *See,* e.g., the annual reports issued by the College Entrance Examination Board from 1972 through 1979 under the title *National College Bound Seniors* (New York: CEEB, 1972-79).

(16) Lerner, 1982, op. cit.

(17) Judith V. Torney, A.N. Oppenheim, & Russell F. Farnen, *Civic Education in Ten Countries: An Empirical Study* (New York: Wiley, 1975); Ralph W. Tyler, "The U.S. vs. the World: A Comparison of Educational Performance, *Phi Delta Kappan,* 1981, 62, 307-310; Richard M. Wolf, *Achievement in America: National Report of the United States for the International Educational Achievement Project* (New York: Teachers College Press, 1977).

(18) Ibid.

(19) Nigel Grant, *Soviet Education,* 4th ed. (New York: Penguin Books, 1979);

mathematician Izaak Wirszup indicates that in the last few years, the Soviet's secondary school graduation rate rose dramatically but there was no comparable increase in the number of Soviet students who go on to college, currently estimated at about one million a year.(20) China, insofar as available data enable us to judge, seems to be graduating less than 20% of her secondary students and to be allowing only about 5% of these – less than 1% of the entire age group – to enter institutions of higher learning. Thus, of some 6 million students who took the newly reinstituted college entrance exam in China in 1978, only about 290,000 were selected for post-secondary education, a selection ratio of about 20 to 1.(21)

Using the same measures – years of schooling completed and/or degrees received – American teachers seem as superior as American students. In the mid-sixties, about 15% of the elementary school teachers and about 30% of the high school teachers in this country held masters or doctors degrees; by 1980, those figures had risen to about 40% and 50%, respectively.(22) Comparisons made by the International Association for the Evaluation of Educational Achievement (IEA) in the 1960s and 70s indicate that no other nation had school teachers with that many years of post-secondary education.(23)

On this basis, it would have seemed reasonable to anticipate high and rising work force productivity in the United States, and great success in meeting foreign competition in economic endeavours, in which large pools of workers and managers with highly developed abilities are a decided asset. In fact, the opposite seems to have happened: American productivity declined sharply, particularly in the 1970s, and American firms experienced increasing difficulty in maintaining their former

Delbert & Roberta Long, *Education in the USSR* (Bloomington, Indiana: Phi Delta Kappa, 1980); Hedrick Smith, *The Russians* (New York: Ballantine Books, 1977) p. 254.

(20) Izaak Wirszup, "The Soviet Challenge," *Educational Leadership,* February 1981.

(21) Robert D. Barendsen, *The 1978 National College Entrance Examination in the People's Republic of China* (Washington, D.C.: U.S. Office of Education, 1979); Fox Butterfield, *China: Alive in the Bitter Sea* (New York: Times Books, 1982), p. 197; Ronald Dore, *The Diploma Disease* (Berkeley: University of California Press, 1976), p. 171.

(22) U.S. Census 1981, op. cit., p. 151.

(23) A. Harry Passow, Harold J. Noah, Max A. Epstein, and John R. Mallea, *The National Case Study: An Empirical Comparative Study of Twenty-one Educational Systems* (New York: John Wiley & Sons, 1976); Torney et al, op. cit., p. 71.

shares of the market, at home and abroad, in a variety of areas where human capital seems to play an important role. In many of those areas, Japanese firms made striking gains, but Swedish firms did not, and countries like West Germany with much smaller proportions of highly schooled workers and managers did not seem unduly handicapped in competition with either the Swedes or the Americans.

3. Test Scores, Occupational Competence, and Productivity

During this same period, predictions made on the basis of test scores would have been very different, particularly in the American case, but few such predictions were made. Here, the problem was not so much a lack of familiarity on the part of economists and others with test results over time; the failure was one of connectedness. Almost all regular readers of the American press are aware that scores on one of the best known standardized tests in routine use in this country – the Scholastic Aptitude Test (SAT) – began to decline in 1964 and continued to do so at a generally accelerating rate for the next 16 years, through 1980.(24) The problem was that few readers had any clear notion of what economic relevance, if any, that had. The economic relevance of literacy seems clear; the economic relevance of the abilities measured by the SAT and a host of similar tests – developed verbal and mathematical reasoning abilities – seems much more obscure, not only to economists but to many psychometricians as well.

Psychometricians are divided by subject matter specialty areas into two main groups, one focusing on educational questions, the other on questions of industrial and organizational psychology. When it comes to methodology, there is much common ground between the two groups; when it comes to substantive ideas, relatively little.

The psychometricians who developed the SAT were educators and educational psychologists, and the concerns of industrial psychologists, were, in many ways, as foreign to them as those of economists. Their exclusive aim, from about 1900 on, was to devise a test that would be useful in predicting a high school

(24) College Board, *On Further Examination: Report of the Advisory Panel on the SAT Score Decline* (New York: College Entrance Examination Board, 1977); College Board, op. cit., 1978, 1979, and 1980.

student's chances for success in college, irrespective of the exact nature of the substantive curriculum in the particular high school he or she had attended.(25) The result of their efforts, the SAT, was first introduced in 1926, and it has been in continuous use ever since, with samples of students that have grown progressively larger over the years. In recent decades, the number of American students taking it each year has ranged from about a million to a million and a half.

From the beginning, the SAT did the job it was intended to do quite well: correlations between high school SAT scores and first year college grades have been consistently significant over the years, no matter what sort of backgrounds the test-takers came from or which academic fields they entered. The usual correlations were and are moderate, not high, but they are, nonetheless, impressive, especially in light of the fact that, until very recently, most schools using the SAT had highly selective admissions policies. Students with low scores were usually denied admission altogether, narrowing the range of scores in the accepted group quite sharply, and making it much harder to get high correlations, even with very large samples, than it is with unselected samples exhibiting the full range of possible scores.(26)

Scholastic predictive power notwithstanding, the link between the abilities measured by the SAT and those required for occupational competence and economic productivity seems, at first glance, to be much weaker. Many educational specialists are unaware that it exists at all, and assume that the abilities needed in the occupational sphere are quite distinct from those needed in the academic one. In fact, however, there is a large and growing mass of empirical evidence indicating that developed verbal and mathematical reasoning abilities are as important in the occupational sphere as they are in the educational one, and that tests of these abilities have comparable predictive power in both spheres. This comparability extends to breadth as well as to height: the predictive power of these tests crosscuts the lines between different jobs as easily as it crosscuts those between different academic fields.

The evidence on this question is derived from a very large

(25) Barbara Lerner, "The War on Testing: David, Goliath, and Gallup." *The Public Interest,* Vol. 60, Summer, 1980b, pp. 126-127.

(26) Ibid., p. 137.

number of studies by industrial psychologists over a period of more than 50 years but, because most of these studies were based on very small samples, their overall import was not clearly perceived, even by industrial psychologists, until quite recently. Results from studies with small samples can be and often are seriously misleading – as misleading, in fact, as those from studies using crude and inaccurate measures. Accurate measures are essential, as illustrated by the example of literacy, but they are not enough. Adequate samples are also necessary for a clear picture of reality to emerge. Studies in industrial psychology often met the first criterion; they seldom met the second.

As a result, industrial psychologists found what looked, to many of them in the 1960s and early 1970s, like an endless array of situation-specific vocational requirements.(27) No single test or group of tests seemed capable of predicting the performance of workers or managers in different lines of work. Worse yet, no single test or group of tests seemed capable of predicting performance in different industrial settings, even when the job titles and descriptions involved were virtually identical. Generality seemed nonexistent; specificity all pervasive.

Methodological developments in the second half of the last decade brought this chaotic picture into sharp and sudden focus. New meta-analytic techniques developed more or less simultaneously by separate groups of educational and industrial psychologists in the late 1970s allowed psychometricians to aggregate data across hundreds of separate small sample studies creating combined sample sizes in the thousands and hundreds of thousands, correcting for the severe deficiencies in sample size that had plagued their work in the past,(28) and in some

(27) L.E. Albright, J.R. Glennon, and W.J. Smith, *The Use of Psychological Tests in Industry* (Cleveland: Howard Allen, 1963), p. 18; E.E. Ghiselli, *The Validity of Occupational Aptitude Tests* (New York: Wiley, 1966), p. 28; Robert M. Guion, *Personnel Testing* (New York: McGraw Hill, 1965), p. 126.

(28) Gene V. Glass, "Primary, Secondary, and Meta-analysis of Research," *Educational Researcher,* 1976, 5, 3-8. Gene V. Glass, "Integrating Findings: The Meta-analysis of Research," *Review of Research in Education,* 1977, 5, 351-379; Gene V. Glass, G. McGaw, and M.L. Smith, *Meta-analysis in Social Research* (Beverly Hills, Calif.: Sage Publications, 1981); John E. Hunter, Frank L. Schmidt, and Gregg B. Jackson, *Meta-analysis: Cumulating Research Findings Across Studies* (Beverly Hills, Calif.: Sage Publications, 1982); Frank L. Schmidt and John E. Hunter, "Development of a General Solution to the Problem of Validity Generalization," *Journal of Applied Psychology,* 1977, 62, 529-540.

cases, making useful corrections for restriction of range and criterion unreliability as well. When these procedures were followed, the apparent variability in results achieved with tests of the predictive power of the same abilities in different situations was revealed to be largely artifactual.

The most impressive large scale research program along these lines was that carried out by Frank Schmidt, John Hunter, and their colleagues. Their pioneering work in the development and application of meta-analytic techniques to the problems of industrial psychology provided us with a series of convincing demonstrations of the fact that tests of verbal and mathematical reasoning ability are at least as powerful in the occupational sphere as they are in the educational arena. These SAT-like tests predict worker competence and productivity in a very wide array of occupations at a very wide range of levels and across a very wide variety of settings.

The Schmidt-Hunter group began their work with statistical analyses demonstrating that the sample sizes needed to produce adequate power in typical empirical validation situations were in the 100 to 1,000 range – much larger than most industrial psychologists had assumed, particularly in private sector research where typical American sample sizes were closer to 40 than to 100 or 1,000.(29) In statistical terms, that fact alone could account for most of the variability in test results from one job setting to another. Relationships between test scores and measures of occupational competence and productivity that show up with great clarity and consistency in samples of 100 to 1,000 would, predictably, be obscured by chance variations in smaller samples, and at predictable frequencies. Examining the literature on situation specificity with this analysis in mind, the Schmidt-Hunter group found that the predicted frequencies of these chance variations were very close to the actual frequencies found in small sample research. Building on this foundation, they emerged with a general solution to the problem of validity generalization(30) and with

(29) Frank L. Schmidt, John E. Hunter, and Vern W. Urry, "Statistical Power in Criterion-Related Validation Studies," *Journal of Applied Psychology,* 1976, 61, 473-485; Frank L. Schmidt and John E. Hunter, "Moderator Research and the Law of Small Numbers," *Personnel Psychology,* 1978, 31, 215-231.

(30) Frank L. Schmidt and John E. Hunter, "Development of a General Solution to the Problem of Validity Generalization," *Journal of Applied Psychology,* 1977, 62, 529-540.

the methodology necessary to test it out by compiling and aggregating data from a multiplicity of small sample studies.(31)

On a more concrete level, they began by focusing on a single job – computer programming – and examining the ability of a particular test – the Programmer Aptitude Test (PAT) – to predict the later competence and productivity of entry-level computer programmers in a variety of different job settings, in the federal government which employed almost 20,000 of them in 1976, and in the U.S. economy as a whole which employed more than 150,000 of them in 1970.(32) The PAT is not as well known as the SAT but it, too, measures mathematical reasoning ability, and it was found to have substantial and generalizable validity in selecting superior performing computer programmers in all work settings studied. The relationship between test scores and occupational competence in this line of work proved to be substantially linear, whether the criterion of competence was success in meeting training program standards or on-the-job performance, and the differences in output between high and low scoring programmers were quite substantial, especially at the extremes. Supervisors estimated the difference in dollar value of output between programmers at the 85th and 50th percentiles at about $10,000 per programmer per year, and the same was true for the difference between programmers at the 50th and 15th percentiles. Extrapolating from these figures, the estimated productivity gains that would have been derived from using the PAT to select all computer programmers would be more than a billion dollars for the federal government alone, more than 10 billion dollars for the U.S. economy as a whole.

Next, the Schmidt-Hunter group focused on clerical work as defined by the U.S. Labor Department's Dictionary of Occupational Titles (DOT)(33) – a large family of different jobs which includes production and stock clerks and computing and account recording clerks as well as the usual typists, stenogra-

(31) See sources cited at n. 28 supra.

(32) Frank L. Schmidt, John E. Hunter, R.C. McKenzie and Tessie W. Muldrow, "The impact of valid selection procedures on work force productivity," *Journal of Applied Psychology*, 1979, 64, 609-626; Frank L. Schmidt, I. Gast-Rosenberg, and John E. Hunter, "Validity Generalization Results for Computer Programmers," *Journal of Applied Psychology*, 1980, 65, 635-642.

(33) U.S. Department of Labor, *Dictionary of Occupational Titles* (4th ed.) (Washington, D.C.: U.S. Government Printing Office, 1977).

phers, and file clerks, among others. A thorough literature search revealed 698 previous psychometric studies relevant to these jobs, studies with a total combined sample size of more than 350,000. These studies had used a variety of different tests, measuring a variety of different abilities. Schmidt and Hunter used meta-analytic techniques to analyze them all, and found that for most clerical jobs, the best predictors of occupational competence were tests of verbal and mathematical reasoning abilities, in combination with tests of perceptual speed and accuracy, and concluded "[r]esults strongly suggested that validities were the same for all clerical occupations despite differences in task make-up among the different areas of clerical work."(34)

Having found powerful evidence for validity generalization for the same job in different settings, and for different jobs in the same job family, the Schmidt-Hunter group then looked at available data on the power of tests of the same abilities to predict competence at different jobs in different job families.(35) For this purpose, they focused on two employment tests that have been used with maximally diverse populations of workers over extended periods of time: the GATB (General Aptitude Test Battery) and the ACB (Army Classification Battery). Sample size is rarely a problem with the ACB or its successor, ASVAB, because the employer who uses them is a very large employer indeed – the U.S. military.(36) It was a problem with the GATB but meta-analytic techniques obviated that problem. Both tests measure developed verbal and mathematical reasoning abilities, as well as some other cognitive attributes, and both are routinely used with workers representing the entire range of occupations in the purview of the testing agency. In case of the GATB, the testing agency is the U.S. Labor

(34) Kenneth Pearlman, Frank L. Schmidt, and John E. Hunter, "Validity Generalization Results for Tests Used to Predict Training Success and Job Proficiency in Clerical Occupations," *Journal of Applied Psychology,* 1980, 65, 373-406.

(35) John E. Hunter, "Validity Generalization for 12,000 Jobs: An Application of Synthetic Validity and Validity Generalization to the General Aptitude Test Battery," U.S. Employment Service, U.S. Department of Labor, Washington D.C. 1980; John E. Hunter, "Validity Generalization and Construct Validity," in *Construct Validity and Psychological Measurement,* Princeton, N.J.: Educational Testing Service, 1980; Frank L. Schmidt, John E. Hunter, and Kenneth Pearlman, "Task Differences in the Validity of Aptitude Tests in Selection: A Red Herring," *Journal of Applied Psychology,* 1981, 66, 166-185.

(36) Lerner, 1980b, op. cit. at p. 125.

Department and its purview is the civilian economy as a whole. The ACB was a U.S. Army classification test, used to help assign soldiers to military jobs as diverse as those of cooks, welders, clerks, radar repairers, personnel administrators and small weapons mechanics.

Massive data from both tests indicate that verbal and mathematical ability scores allow us to predict the occupational competence of workers in all jobs studied, military and civilian, at a level well beyond chance. The number of jobs studied was very large: in the army study, 35 different jobs were involved; in the Labor Department study, 500 different jobs. As might be expected, the correlations between verbal and mathematical reasoning abilities and occupational competence were highest for managerial and professional jobs, lowest for semi-skilled and unskilled ones, but even in the latter case, they were still high enough to have practical impact. For skilled workers, white collar or blue, the correlations were highest for jobs like repairman in which problem-solving is an essential element; lowest for jobs like dental hygienist in which routine procedures are routinely followed.

These results surprised many psychometricians, but should not have. The data on ACB scores and occupational competence reported by Schmidt and Hunter were collected when those two researchers were still schoolboys. It comes from a 1957 military study with sample sizes so large that no newly developed methodological refinements were needed to uncover its essential implications.(37) Similar samples are the rule rather than the exception for military testing and have been throughout its history, a history that extends back in time to World War I. Similar results are the rule, too. Here, for example, is the testimony of a distinguished veteran psychometrician, Professor Lloyd G. Humphreys of the University of Illinois, summarizing his experiences, first as a member of the U.S. Air Force's Aviation Psychology Program in the 1940s and then as a civilian director of the Air Force Research Unit in the 1950s:

> In summary, therefore, the primary problem was finding stable differential validities for the tests we were administering. Establishing validity generalization [for tests of

(37) W.E. Helm, W.A. Gibson, and H.E. Brogden, "An Empirical Test of Shrinkage Problems in Personnel Classification Research," Adjunct General's Office, Personnel Research Board Technical Research Report, Note 84, October, 1957.

verbal and mathematical reasoning abilities] was no problem; it could not be avoided. (38)

4. Test Scores and Economic Realities Across Space

The evidence summarized above indicates that scores on standardized tests of verbal and mathematical reasoning abilities relate to economic competence and productivity in meaningful ways. As such, they provide a potentially useful alternative to traditional measures of economically relevant higher abilities like "years of schooling completed," or "diplomas received." They provide an alternative picture of the development of human capital in the world in the 1960s and 70s too, a picture that is sharply at odds with the one painted by traditional measures, but one that seems much more compatible with emerging economic realities.

This alternative picture is still very incomplete, because instances when representative samples of populations from different nations take the same tests are still relatively rare, especially in vocational as opposed to academic settings. As a result, there are little or no useful comparative test data on the scores of workers in different nations, or, at any rate, little or none in the public domain. Cross-national coverage is better for student samples, but even in this area, large gaps remain. We have, for example, no useful comparative data at all on the scores of Russian or Chinese students, and that is true for students from most developing nations as well.

We do, however, have some data on the scores of students in at least two eastern bloc countries – Hungary and Rumania – and on students in at least four developing countries – Chile, India, Iran, and Thailand. The data base for developed nations in the noncommunist world is much more complete: we have some good initial comparative data on students from the United States, Japan, and Sweden, and from most other western European nations as well, including England, Scotland, Ireland, France, West Germany, Italy, Belgium, and the Netherlands.

These data were collected by an international group of educators and educational psychologists working first in connection with UNESCO and later under the auspices of the IEA

(38) Lloyd G. Humphreys, Unpublished Memorandum on Validity Generalization, University of Illinois in Urbana, 1982.

– the International Association for the Evaluation of Educational Achievement. Beginning in the late 1950s, these researchers worked together to develop a battery of international tests, many available in as many as 14 different languages. In the late 1960s and the early 1970s, varying parts of this test battery were administered to reasonably large, representative samples of students from a total of 21 countries – more than a quarter of a million students in all. (39) We also have interesting additional data specific to comparisons between students from the United States and Puerto Rico, derived from an equating study of the Prueba de Aptitud Academica – the Spanish-language version of the SAT. (40)

The SAT is, of course, a direct test of developed verbal and mathematical reasoning abilities, as were three of the eight tests developed by the IEA. The other five IEA tests covered substantive knowledge in a variety of specific content areas – science, literature, civics, and two "foreign" languages, French and English. Tests of the latter type are generally referred to as

(39) For useful overviews, analyses, and critiques of the IEA studies, *see* Lerner, 1982, op. cit.; Alex Inkeles, "The International Evaluation of Educational Achievement: A Review," *Proceedings of the National Academy of Education,* Vol. 4, 1977, pp. 139-200; Alan C. Purves and Daniel U. Levine, *Educational Policy and Internation Assessment: Implications of the IEA Surveys of Achievement* (Berkeley, California: McCutchan, 1975).

For the IEA's own reports on the data collected, *see* John B. Carroll, *The Teaching of French as a Foreign Language in Eight Countries* (New York: Wiley, 1975); L.C. Comber and John P. Keeves, *Science Education in Nineteen Countries: An Empirical Study* (New York: Wiley, 1973); Torsten Husen (Ed), *International Study of Achievement in Mathematics: A Comparison of Twelve Countries,* Vols. I and II (New York: Wiley, 1967); E. Glyn Lewis and Carolyn E. Massad, *The Teaching of English as a Foreign Language in Ten Countries* (New York: Wiley, 1975); A Harry Passow, Harold J. Noah, Max A. Eckstein, and John R. Mallea, *The National Case Study: An Empirical Comparative Study of Twenty-One Educational Systems* (New York: Wiley, 1976); Gilbert F. Peaker, *An Empirical Study of Education in Twenty-one Countries: A Technical Report* (New York: Wiley, 1975); Alan C. Purves, *Literature Education in Ten Countries: An Empirical Study* (New York: Wiley, 1973); Robert L. Thorndike, *Reading Comprehension Education in Fifteen Countries: An Empirical Study* (New York: Wiley, 1973); Judith V. Torney, A.N. Oppenheim, and Russell F. Farnen, *Civic Education in Ten Countries: An Empirical Study* (New York: Wiley, 1975); and David A. Walker, *The IEA Six-Subject Survey: An Empirical Study of Education in Twenty-one Countries* (New York: Wiley, 1976).

See also Richard D. Noonan, *School Resources, Social Class, and Student Achievement* (New York: Wiley, 1976).

(40) William H. Angoff and Christopher C. Modu, Equating the Scales of the Spanish-Language Prueba de Aptitud Academica and the English-language Scholastic Aptitude Test of the College Entrance Examination Board (New York: CEEB Research and Development Report 72-73, No. 4, January 1973).

knowledge or achievement tests, and previous research on the relationship between tests of that type and tests of verbal and mathematical reasoning abilities indicates that correlations between the two are generally high, making it reasonable to combine data on both types of test in making a rough initial assessment of the relative levels of human capital development in different countries during the last two decades.

Combined data from these sources strongly suggest that it was Japan and not the United States that led the world in the development of human capital in the late 1960s and in the early 1970s. In the IEA studies, Japanese students participated in tests of mathematical reasoning ability and in tests of knowledge in the physical and biological sciences, and their mean scores were dramatically higher than those of American students on both types of test. Japanese students' mean scores on these tests also surpassed those of students from most western European nations most of the time.

Students from western European nations also surpassed students from the United States, not all of the time as in the case of Japan, but most of the time and, in general, the older the students, the greater the gap. Even Swedish students, who ranked in the bottom half of the western European distribution more often than not, surpassed American students on most tests at most age and grade levels. Hungarian and Rumanian students, on the other hand, generally seemed to do about as well as students from western European nations and, in at least one instance, markedly better.

The only student group whose test score means were usually lower than those of American students in the 1960s and 70s were those from underdeveloped nations. On the IEA tests, students from those nations generally had mean scores that were about two standard deviations below those of students from developed nations. In contrast, the usual maximum gap between the test score means of students from different developed nations was only half as large – about one standard deviation.(41)

(41) *See* Lerner, 1982, op. cit. at p. 64. *See also* Benjamin S. Bloom, "Implications of the IEA Studies for Curriculum and Instruction" at p. 68 in Purves and Levine, op. cit.

5. Test Scores and Economic Realities Over Time

The gross, immediate economic predictions one would make on the basis of the over-all international test score pattern presented above seem clear. Japan would be expected to lead the world in economic growth, at least, to the extent that economic growth is dependent on the development of human capital. In this rank order, Europe would be second, followed by the United States, and then the less developed nations. The fit between these predictions and the economic realities of the last decade or so seems reasonably close, especially when compared to the predictions suggested by the traditional measures of human capital at this level.

Those traditional measures – years of schooling completed and/or degrees received – did not reflect the full magnitude of Japanese progress in the development of human capital in the post World War II years, and they did not reflect America's backward movement at all. Test scores did, showing large gains in Japan,(42) and even larger losses in the United States.(43)

This gross difference in the sensitivity of the two types of measures is not as surprising as it may at first appear. Scores on well-constructed standardized tests have a great advantage over the traditional measures of human capital when it comes to detecting and measuring changes over time. They allow us to measure them with a high degree of accuracy because they allow us to maintain a relatively constant standard over time, and to detect and measure any shifts in standards that do occur.

Thus, in the American case, research on scale drift with the SAT shows that efforts to hold the difficulty level of the test constant over the years were quite successful from 1941 to 1963.(44) Efforts were somewhat less successful from 1963 to 1973, when some downward drift occurred, making it a bit easier to get higher scores after 1963 than before.(45) The SAT

(42) Richard Lynn, "I.Q. in Japan and the United States Shows a Growing Disparity," *Nature,* Vol. 297, pp. 222-223, May, 1982; Lester Tarnopol and Muriel Tarnopol, "Arithmetic Ability in Chinese and Japanese Children," *Focus on Learning Problems in Mathematics,* Vol. 2, pp. 29-48, July, 1980.

(43) Lerner, 1982, op. cit.

(44) E.E. Stewart, The Stability of the SAT-Verbal Score Scale, College Entrance Examination Board Research and Development Report 667, No. 3 (Princeton, N.J.: Educational Testing Service, 1966).

(45) Christopher C. Modu and June Stern, The Stability of the SAT-Verbal Score Scale, Report for the Advisoty Panel on the SAT Score Decline (New York: College Entrance Examination Board, 1977).

was also easier to read in the 1960s and 70s than it was in the 1940s and 50s: the difficulty level of reading passages on the test declined, as measured by the Dale-Chall formula, from a corrected grade level of 13-15 to one of only 11-12.(46) All in all, SAT scores in recent decades probably underestimate the actual American score decline by about 8 to 12 points.(47)

These minor shifts in constancy of measurement might have obscured a minor negative change in the level of development of the verbal and mathematical reasoning abilities of American students, but they did not obscure the major negative change that took place here in the 1960s and 70s the way traditional measures did. Traditional measures indicated that American competence levels were going up. Scale drift notwithstanding, SAT data indicated that the mean scores of American students declined by some 90 points from 1963 to 1980,(48) a drop that is in the neighborhood of one half of a standard deviation. All in all, test scores seem to have a better track record as measures of human capital and as predictors of economic growth and development. Still, all this is post hoc prediction, an art with limited validity and utility.

Let us now examine American test score patterns over time in more detail, in an effort to see the past more clearly, and to tease out some initial a priore predictions. For this purpose, we shall focus mainly on the SAT, because it is one of the few good tests in common use in this country for which we have sufficiently detailed data on year-to-year changes in mean scores over a long enough period of time to make a detailed examination of patterns of temporal change feasible.

The SAT, as noted in section 3, has been in continuous, annual use with samples of American high school students who plan to go on to colleges, particularly eastern ones, since 1926 but, unfortunately, the owner of the test, the College Entrance Examination Board, has seen fit to release annual mean scores only from 1952 onwards. Still, that leaves us with data on year-

(46) Jeanne S. Chall, An Analysis of Textbooks in Relation to Declining SAT Scores. Report for the Advisory Panel on the SAT Score Decline (New York: College Entrance Examination Board, 1977).

(47) College Entrance Examination Board, On Further Examination, op. cit. at p. 9.

(48) In 1963, the year before the decline began, the mean SAT-V score was 478 and the mean SAT-M score was 502. By 1980, the mean SAT-V score had fallen 54 points to 424, and the mean SAT-M score had fallen 36 points to 466. See Sources cited at n. 24 supra.

to-year changes over a period of 30 years, from 1952 to 1982, as of this writing, and provides at least a starting point for analyses of patterns of change and predictions based on them.

These data reveal that SAT mean scores were quite stable in this country from at least 1952 through 1963, varying by only a few points from one typical year to the next, and going up about as often as down. This was true on the verbal reasoning part of the test, the SAT-V, and on the mathematical reasoning part, the SAT-M, and it was true for total combined scores as well. The largest, single year-to-year change in mean scores on either the SAT-V or the SAT-M during this period was 6 points; the smallest was zero – on a scoreboard that runs from 200 points to 800. For combined scores, the range of year-to-year changes was from zero to 11 points.

This period of stability ended, as we can see clearly, in retrospect, in 1964, when means scores on both halves of the test began to go down, and continued to do so for a total of 17 almost-consecutive years. The one exception, the "almost," was in the 1976-77 period when scores on the SAT-M went up by 1 point. This dramatic, overall shift in direction was not, however, accompanied by any dramatic shift in the magnitude of year-to-year changes or, indeed, by any substantial changes in these magnitudes at all. From 1964 to 1980, the largest year-to-year change in SAT-V scores was 8 points; the smallest was zero. The range of change score magnitudes on the SAT-M was even smaller from 5 points to, again, zero. For combined scores, the range was similarly unchanged, from zero to 11 points.

This long, slow slide seems large enough to have the kind of cumulative economic impact suggested for it here, particularly in light of the fact that declines on the SAT were parallelled by declines of comparable magnitude on the battery of knowledge tests administered by the ACT(49) – the Iowa based American

(49) Albert E. Beaton, Thomas L. Hilton, and William B. Schrader, Changes in the Verbal Abilities of High School Seniors, College Entrants, and SAT Candidates between 1960 and 1972, Report for the Advisory Panel on the SAT Score Decline (New York: College Entrance Examination Board, 1977); Hunter Breland, The SAT Score Decline: A Summary of Related Research, Report for the Advisory Panel on the SAT Score Decline (New York: CEEB, 1976); T. Anne Cleary and Sam A. McCandless, Summary of Score Changes in Other Tests, Report for the Advisory Panel on the SAT Score Decline (New York: CEEB, 1977).

For evidence of declines on other tests from grade 5 onward, see Lerner, 1982, op. cit. Paul Copperman, "The Achievement Decline of the 1970s," *Phi Delta Kappan* 60, p. 736, June, 1979; Annegret Harnischfeger and David E. Wiley, Achieve-

College Testing Program – and taken, in recent years, by about a half million prospective college entrants a year, in the midwest and, increasingly, in other parts of the nation as well. Of course, neither SAT nor ACT-takers are random samples of America's high school population or of her potential labor force as a whole. Taken together, however, the one and one-half million or so American 17 and 18 year olds who take these tests each year do constitute a reasonably adequate rough sample of the potential managerial, professional, and scientific replacement pool that America generated in the late 1960s and in the 1970s.

This pool, as we saw in Section 2 on traditional measures of higher abilities, was greatly expanded in the 1960s when the proportion of American high school graduates entering college rose dramatically. However, the great American score decline cannot really be explained away on that basis, for two compelling reasons. First, the expansion levelled off in the 1970s, but the decline did not; it accelerated.(50) Second, the decline was not just in the proportion of high scoring students but in the absolute numbers of them as well: there were fewer American 17 and 18 year olds with scores over 600 on either the verbal or the mathematical part of the SAT in the 1970s than there were in the 1950s.(51)

Something similar seems to surface in one of the few comparisons we have between American students in the 1970s and their predecessors in the 1920s.(52) In 1928, a 25-year old research assistant named Alvin C. Eurich prepared one of the early standardized tests of verbal reasoning abilities and administered it to high school seniors and to college freshmen in the

ment Test Score Decline: Do We Need to Worry? (Chicago: CEMREL, 1975); Wayne H. Martin, "National Assessment of Educational Progress," pp. 45-68 in John E. Milholland (Ed.), *New Directions for Testing and Measurement: Insights From Large Scale Surveys* (San Francisco: Jossey-Bass, 1979).

(50) Rex Jackson, A Summary of SAT Score Statistics for College Board Candidates. Report for the Advisory Panel on the SAT Score Decline (New York: College Entrance Examination Board, 1976a); Rex Jackson, An Examination of Declining Numbers of High-Scoring SAT Candidates, Report for the Advisory Panel on the SAT Score Decline (New York: College Entrance Examination Board, 1976b); D. Perry and E.O. Swanson, "Decline in Minnesota College Aptitude Test Scores," in J. Fasold (Ed.), *Decline in Standardized Test Scores: A Widespread Phenomenon* (Salem, Oregon: Oregon Department of Education, 1974).

(51) See sources cited at n. 50, supra.

(52) Fred M. Hechinger, "1978 Freshman Score Poorly on 1928 Exam," *New York Times,* March 18, 1980, p. C1.

state of Minnesota. In 1978, he readministered it to samples of students drawn from the same schools. He compared students whose scores placed them in the top 1%, then and now, and found that in 1978, no student scored above 75 on this test – a drop of 20 points from the highest scores in 1928. Only one student out of 100 scored near 60 in 1978; 5 out of 100 did so in 1928.

What all of this suggests is that America may have entered a period in which high level managerial, professional, and scientific talent will be in short supply, a period when her stock of developed human capital is lower than it has been in the past, and in need of replenishing. How quickly can that be done? Available data reviewed above suggest that the average past rate of change was about 5 points a year, the maximum rate about 10 points. Thus, even if we assume that the decline ended in 1981 – and the evidence for that is, as yet, far from conclusive(53) – and that replenishment occurs at the maximum past rate, it would still take about 10 years before the scores of America's leadership replacement pool return to their former levels. This situation is likely to cause continuing economic problems for the United States until at least 1990, and perhaps beyond; it will, of course, pose challenging social and political problems, too.

The seriousness of these problems will depend, in part, on domestic factors: chiefly, the size of the cohorts involved and the efficacy of the steps taken to improve the performance of the affected cohorts, and of their successors. Improving the performance of successor generations is obviously important, but it will probably not, in and of itself, be enough to offset losses because of the size of the affected cohorts. The affected cohorts – Americans who came of age in the latter half of the 1960s and in the 1970s, for the most part – are the products

(53) In 1981, scores were the same as in 1980; in 1982, they rose by 3 points. See *College Bound Seniors,* 1981 & 1982 (New York: College Board). Obviously, two in a row is not yet a trend, but there do seem to be good theoretical reasons to expect improvements in functional literacy rates and, perhaps, in the development of higher level abilities as well. See Barbara Lerner, "The Minimum Competence Testing Movement: Social, Scientific, and Legal Implications," *American Psychologist,* October, 1981, pp. 1057-1066; Barbara Lerner, *Minimum Competence, Maximum Choice: Second Chance Legislation* (New York: Irvington, 1980). And, the experience of America's ethnic groups, as Thomas Sowell has shown, provide ample precedent for striking gains over time. See Sowell, "Assumptions versus History in Ethnic Education," *Teachers College Record,* Fall, 1981, pp. 37-71.

of the post World War II baby boom in this country, and they are very large cohorts indeed, in both absolute and proportional terms.(54) As a result, the potential impact of retraining will also be unusually large, and it will be needed at the bottom level, to reduce the number of illiterate and semi-literate Americans as well as at the top level, to sharpen the abilities of America's younger managers, professionals, and scientists.

Domestic factors notwithstanding, the seriousness of America's human capital problems in the 1980s and beyond will also be determined, in substantial part; by patterns of human capital development in the rest of the world. Here, the examples provided by the United States and Japan should caution us against any automatic assumptions about the stability of the international patterns recorded on IEA tests in the late 1960s and the early 1970s. In both countries, domestic data on test score patterns over time highlight the prominence of change, and there is no good reason to assume that similar changes, up or down, will not occur in other nations – perhaps even in whole regions of the world – in the waning decades of this century. Some may already have occurred, and/or be in process. Thus, it is possible that the score decline reached western Europe, too, but with a bit of a time lag, as many cultural phenomena do, and there are some interesting non-psychometric indications that, for reasons of her own, the USSR may also be struggling with problems of human capital, and of standards. Certainly, post-cultural revolution China is, and, although we have no relevant test data to support it, it is a safe prediction that the Chinese problem is an especially formidable one.(55)

The work upon which this publication is based was performed pursuant to the Contract No. NIE-P-82-0088 of the National Institute of Education. It does not, however, necessarily reflect the views of that agency.

(54) The absolute size of cohorts born in the past is, of course, a known quantity, but their relative size depends, in part, on current and future birthrates. Updated census projections relevant to the latter are due out in March, 1983.

(55) Butterfield, op. cit., Simon Leys, *Chinese Shadows* (New York: Penguin, 1978).

REFERENCES

Adelson, Joseph
1983 Twenty-five years of American Education: An Interpretation. Report to the Commission on Excellence. Washington, D.C.: U.S. Office of Education.

Albright, L.E., J.R. Glennon and W.J. Smith
1963 Use of Psychological Tests in Industry. Cleveland: Howard Allen.

Angoff, William H. and Christopher C. Modu
1973 Equating the Scales of the Spanish-Language Prueba de Aptitud Academica and the English-Language Scholastic Aptitude Test of the College Entrance Examination Board. New York: College Board Research and Development Report 72-73, No. 4.

Armbruster, Frank and Paul J. Bracken
1975 The U.S. Primary and Secondary Education Process. Croton-on-Hudson, New York: Hudson Institute.

Barendsen, Robert D.
1979 The 1978 National College Entrance Examination in the People's Republic of China. Washington, D.C.: U.S. Office of Education.

Beaton, Albert E., Thomas L. Hilton and William B. Schrader
1977 Changes in the Verbal Abilities of High School Seniors, College Entrants, and SAT Candidates between 1960 and 1972. Report for the Advisoty Panel on the SAT Score Decline. New York: College Board.

Bjork, Robert M. and Stewart E. Fraser
1980 Population, Education, and Children's Futures. Bloomington, Indiana: Phi Delta Kappa.

Bloom, Benjamin S.
1975 Implications of the IEA Studies for Curriculum and Instruction, pp. 65-83 in Alan C. Purves and Daniel U. Levine (Eds.), Education Policy and International Assessment. Berkeley, California: McCutchan.

Breland, Hunter
1976 The SAT Score Decline: A Summary of Related Research. Report for the Advisory Panel on the SAT Score Decline. New York: College Board.

Butterfield, Fox
1982 China: Alive in the Bitter Sea. New York: Times Books.

Carp, Abraham
1971 The Reading Problem in the United States, pp. 36-45 in Reginald Corder, (ed.), The Information Base for Reading: A Critical View of the Information Base for Current Assumptions Regarding the Status of Instruction and Achievement in Reading in the United States. Washington, D.C.: U.S. Office of Education.

Carroll, John B.
1975 The Teaching of French as a Foreign Language in Eight Countries. New York: Wiley.

Chall, Jeanne S.
1977 An Analysis of Textbooks in Relation to Declining SAT Scores. Report for the Advisory Panel on the SAT Score Decline. New York: College Board.

Cleary, T. Anne, and Sam A. McCandless
1977 Summary of Score Changes in Other Tests. Report for the Advisory Panel on the SAT Score Decline. New York: College Board.

College Board
1977 On Further Examination. Report of the Advisory Panel on the SAT Score Decline. New York: College Board.
1972-1982 National College-Bound Seniors (Annual Reports). New York: College Board.

Comber, L.C. and John P. Keeves
1973 Science Education in Nineteen Countries: An Empirical Study. New York: Wiley.

Copperman, Paul
1979 The Achievement Decline of the 1970s *Phi Delta Kappan* 60 (June): 736.

Dore, Ronald
1976 The Diploma Disease. Berkeley: University of California Press.

Ghiselli, Edwin E.
1966 The Validity of Occupational Aptitude Tests. New York: Wiley.

Glass, Gene V., B. McGaw and M.L. Smith
1981 Meta-analysis in Social Research. Beverly Hills, California: Sage.

Glass, Gene V.
1977 Integrating Findings: The Meta-analysis of Research. *Review of Research in Education,* 5: 351-379.
1976 Primary, Secondary and Meta-analysis of Research. *Educational Researcher,* 5:3-8.

Grant, Nigel
1979 Soviet Education (4th Ed.). New York: Penguin.

Guion, Robert M.
1965 Personnel Testing. New York: McGraw-Hill.

Harnischfeger, Annagret and David E. Wiley
1976 Achievement Test Scores Drop. So What? *Educational Researcher* 5: 5-12.
1975 Achievement Test Score Decline: Do We Need to Worry? Chicago: CEMREL.

Harris, Louis and Associates, Inc.
1971 The 1971 National Reading Difficulty Index. Princeton, N.J.: ERIC ED 057 312.
1970 Survival Literacy Study, No. 2036. Washington, D.C.: National Reading Council.

Hechinger, Fred M.
1980 1978 Freshmen Score Poorly on 1928 Exam. *New York Times,* 19 March, p. C1.

Helm, W.E., W.A. Gibson and H.E. Brogden
1957 An Empirical Test of Shrinkage Problems in Personnel Classification Research. Personnel Research Board Technical Research Report, Note 84 (October). Washington, D.C.: Adjunct General's Office.

Hilton, Thomas L.
1979 ETS Study of Academic Prediction and Growth, pp. 27-44 in John E. Milholland (Ed.), New Directions for Testing and Measurement: Insights from Large Scale Surveys. San Francisco: Jossey-Bass.

Humphreys, Lloyd G.
1982 Memorandum on Validity Generalization. Unpublished Manuscript.

Hunter, John E., Frank L. Schmidt and Gregg B. Jackson
1982 Meta-analysis: Cumulating Research Findings Across Studies. Beverly Hills, California: Sage.

Hunter, John E.
1980a Validity Generalization for 12,000 Jobs: An Application of Synthetic Validity and Validity Generalization to the General Aptitude Test Battery (GATB). Washington, D.C.: U.S. Employment Service, U.S. Department of Labor.
1980b Validity Generalization and Construct Validity. In Construct Validity in Psychological Measurement. Princeton, N.J.: Educational Testing Service.

Husen, Torsten (Ed.)
1967 International Study of Achievement in Mathematics: A Comparison of Twelve Countries (Vols. I and II). New York: Wiley.

Inkeles, Alex
1977 The International Evaluation of Educational Achievement: A Review. In *Proceedings of the National Academy of Education,* Vol. 4, pp. 139-200.

Jackson, Rex
1976a A Summary of SAT Score Statistics for College Board Candidates. Report for the Advisory Panel on the SAT Score Decline. New York: College Board.
1976b An Examination of Declining Numbers of High-Scoring SAT Candidates. Report for the Advisory Panel on the SAT Score Decline. New York: College Board.

Lerner, Barbara
1982 American Education: How Are We Doing? *The Public Interest* 69: 59-82.
1981a The Minimum Competence Testing Movement: Social, Scientific, and Legal Implications. *American Psychologist* 36: 1057-1066.
1981b Vouchers for Literacy: Second Chance Legislation. *Phi Delta Kappan* (December): 252-255.

1980a Minimum Competence, Maximum Choice: Second Chance Legislation. New York: Irvington.

1980b The War on Testing: David, Goliath, and Gallup. *The Public Interest* 60: 119-147.

Lewis, E. Glyn and Carolyn E. Massad

1975 The Teaching of English as a Foreign Language in Ten Countries. New York: Wiley.

Leys, Simon

1978 Chinese Shadows. New York: Penguin.

Long, Delbert and Roberta Long

1980 Education in the U.S.S.R. Bloomington, Indiana: Phi Delta Kappa.

Lynn, Richard

1982 I.Q. in Japan and the United States Shows a Growing Disparity. *Nature* 297 (May): 222-223.

Martin, Wayne H.

1979 National Assessment of Educational Progress, pp. 45-68 in John E. Milholland (Ed.), New Directions for Testing and Measurements: Insights from Large Scale Surveys. San Francisco: Jossey-Bass.

Modu, Christopher C. and June Stern

1977 The Stability of the SAT-Verbal Score Scale. Report for the Advisory Panel on the SAT Score Decline. New York: College Board.

Murphy, Richard T.

1973 Adult Functional Reading Study. Washington, D.C.: National Institute of Education.

National Assessment of Educational Progress

1976 Functional Literacy: Basic Reading Performance. Denver, Colorado: NAEP.

Noonan, Richard D.

1976 School Resources, Social Class, and Sudent Achievement. New York: Wiley.

Northcutt, N.

1975 Adult Functional Competency: A Summary. Austin, Texas: University of Texas.

Passow, A. Harry, Harold J. Noah, Max A. Eckstein and John R. Mallea

1976 The National Case Study: An Empirical Comparative Study of Twenty-One Educational Systems. New York: Wiley.

Peaker, Gilbert F.

1975 An Empirical Study of Education in Twenty-one Countries: A Technical Report. New York: Wiley.

Pearlman, Kenneth, Frank L. Schmidt and John E. Hunter

1980 Validity Generalization Results for Tests Used to Predict Training Success and Job Proficiency in Clerical Occupations. *Journal of Applied Psychology* 65: 373-406.

Perry, D. and E.O. Swanson

1974 Decline in Minnesota College Aptitude Test Scores. In J. Fasold et al (Eds), Decline in Standardized Test Scores: A

Widespread Phenomenon. Salem, Oregon: Oregon Department of Education.

Purves, Alan C. and Daniel U. Levine
1975 Educational Policy and International Assessment: Implications of the IEA Surveys of Achievement. Berkeley, California: McCutchan.

Purves, Alan C.
1973 Literature Education in Ten Countries: An Empirical Study. New York: Wiley.

Schmidt, Frank L., John E. Hunter and Kenneth Pearlman
1981 Task Differences and Validity of Aptitude Tests in Selection: A Red Herring. *Journal of Applied Psychology* 66: 166-185.

Schmidt, Frank L., Ilene Gast-Rosenberg and John E. Hunter
1980 Validity Generalization Results for Computer Programmers. *Journal of Applied Psychology* 65: 643-661.

Schmidt, Frank L., John E. Hunter, R.C. McKenzie and T.W. Muldrow
1979 Impact of Valid Selection Procedures on Work-Force Productivity. *Journal of Applied Psychology* 64: 609-626.

Schmidt, Frank L. and John E. Hunter
1978 Moderator Research and the Law of Small Numbers. *Personnel Psychology* 31: 215-232.
1977 Development of a General Solution to the Problem of Validity Generalization. *Journal of Applied Psychology* 62: 529-540.

Schmidt, Frank L., John E. Hunter and Vern W. Urry
1976 Statistical Power in Criterion-Related Validation Studies. *Journal of Applied Psychology* 61: 473-485.

Sivard, Ruth L.
1978 World Military and Social Expenditures 1978. Leesburg, Virginia: WMSE Publications.

Smith, Hedrick
1977 The Russians. New York: Ballantine.

Stewart, E.E.
1966 The Stability of the SAT-Verbal Score Scale. CEEB Research and Development Report 667, No. 3. Princeton, N.J.: Educational Testing Service.

Sticht, T.G., J.S. Caylor, R.P. Kern and L.C. Fox
1972 Project REALISTIC: Determination of Adult Functional Literacy Levels. *Reading Research Quarterly* 7: 424-465.

Sowell, Thomas
1981 Assumptions versus History in Ethnic Education. *Teachers College Record,* (Fall) 37-71.

Tarnopol, Lester and Muriel Tarnopol
1980 Arithmetic Ability in Chinese and Japanese Children. *Focus on Learning Problems in Mathematics* 2: 29-48.

Thorndike, Robert L.
1973 Reading Comprehension Education in Fifteen Countries: An Empirical Study. New York: Wiley.

Torney, Judity V., A.N. Oppenheim and Russell F. Farnen
1975 Civic Education in Ten Countries: An Empirical Study. New York: Wiley.

Tyler, Ralph W.
1981 The U.S. vs. the World: A Comparison of Educational Performance. *Phi Delta Kappan* 62: 307-310.

U.S. Census Bureau
1981 Statistical Abstract of the United States. Washington, D.C.: Government Printing Office.
1975 Historical Statistics of the United States: Colonial Times to 1970, Parts I and II. Washington, D.C.: Government Printing Office.

U.S. Labor Department
1977 Dictionary of Occupational Titles (4th Ed.). Washington, D.C.: Government Printing Office.

Walker, David A.
1976 The IEA Six-Subject Survey: An Empirical Study of Education in Twenty-one Countries. New York: Wiley.

Weber, Rose-Marie
1975 Adult Illiteracy in the United States. In John B. Carroll and Jeanne Chall (Eds.) Toward a Literate Society. New York: McGraw-Hill.

Wirszup, Izaak
1981 The Soviet Challenge. Educational Leadership (February).

Wolf, Richard M.
1977 Achievement in America: National Report of the United States for the International Educational Achievement Project. New York: Teachers College Press.

FERTILITY DIFFERENTIALS AND THE STATUS OF NATIONS: A SPECULATIVE ESSAY ON JAPAN AND THE WEST

DANIEL R. VINING, JR.
University of Pennsylvania

> My thesis [is] that all women, under modern conditions, cease to be cohesive. - Brooks Adams

The study of international variation in human achievement presents many difficulties, not the least of which is that the best hypotheses may lie in realms of inquiry which are now taboo. Perhaps the best initial way of approaching such a field is by taking the strictly empirical approach – or by following now neglected paths laid down by previous generations of scholars, who appear to have enjoyed a greater freedom of expression than our own. I shall employ here both approaches.

The fascination of this subject lies in the unstable nature of the variation. No nation has ever achieved permanent pre-eminence in the world. If one had, the subject would almost certainly not exert the fascination it so manifestly does. So one must explain not only how preeminence is achieved and maintained but how and why it is so regularly lost.

Fisher's Model of National Decay

R.A. Fisher devoted an essay and part of a book to this last question: why do civilizations inevitably fall into decay? (Fisher 1926, 1958) "Bearing in mind the unquestionable advantages of superior knowledge, of coordinated efforts and of industrial skill, should we not confidently anticipate," asked Fisher, "if we were ignorant of the actual history of our planet, that the history of civilization would consist of an unbroken series of triumphs, and that once the germ of an organized society has made its appearance in Babylonia, perhaps, or in Egypt, it would only be a question of time for every country in the world to be in turn absorbed and organized by the Babylonian, or Egyptian, civilization?" Fisher answered himself as follows: "The indications which we possess of the earlier civilizations, as well as the plain narrative of the historic period, differs strangely from the naif yet rational anticipations outlined above." Though we "see, indeed, a certain tenuous continuity of traditional civilization ... [t]he experiment of becoming civilized has, in fact, been performed repeatedly, by peoples of different racial origins, ... and in all cases without exception, if we set aside the incomplete experiment of our own civilization, after a period of glory and domination accompanied by notable contributions to the sciences and arts, they have failed, not only to maintain their national superiority, but even to establish a permanent mediocrity among the nations of the globe ..." (Fisher 1926, p. 129) "To what ought we to ascribe this failure, again and again experienced by the highly civilized nations?" Fisher asked. He rejected failures in civil and political institutions as well as environmental and resource crises as possible causes; to Fisher, these were symptoms rather than causes of national decay. "Peoples in the prime of their powers appear to find no difficulty in making good use of very inferior natural resources, and adapt their national organization with complete success to much more violent changes than those that can be adduced to explain the misfortunes of the later stages of their civilization." (p. 130) The phenomenon of national decay is too regular, too uniform across time and space to admit of many different kinds of causes. "A physician observing a number of patients to sicken and die in similar though not identical conditions, and with similar though not identical symtoms, would surely make an initial error if he did not seek for a single common cause of the disorder. The complexity of the symptoms, and of the disturbances of the various organs of the body, should not lead him to assume that the original cause, or the appropriate remedial measures, must be equally complex. Is this not because the physician assumes that the workings of the body, though immensely complex, are self-regulatory and capable of a normal corrective response to all ordinary disturbances; while only a small number of disturbances of an exceptional kind meet with no effective response and cause severe illness? Have we not equally a right to assume a self-regulatory power in human societies? If not, we should be led to think that such societies should break down under the influence of any of the innumerable accidents to which they are exposed. Human societies of various kinds have adapted themselves to every climate, from the Arctic to the forests and deserts of the Tropics. They share the territories of the most savage or the most poisonous animals, and often long withstand without disruption the assaults of most implacable human enemies. That civilized men, possessed of more effective appliances, with access to more knowledge, and organized for the most detailed co-operation, should prove themselves incapable of effective response to any disturbance of their social organizations, surely demands some very special explanation."

Fisher believed he had found this "very special explanation" in the differential birth rate. First, he observed that birth rates are and have been for some decades running back into the 19th century inversely related to social class and income. These were facts, observables (see, for example, Table 1). Assuming that a civilization is created and maintained due to the high average mental qualities of its citizens and assuming further that such qualities are higher, the higher the social and economic class, on average, and finally assuming that mental qualities of parent and child are positively and strongly correlated, then clearly an inverse relationship between social status and fertility, by lowering the average mental endowment of the population, could weaken the foundations of the civilization which depends on this endowment as on nothing else, eventually causing it to succumb to such immediate disturbances as environmental crises, foreign invasions, resource depletion, etc.

	Social Class	Surviving Children per Married Couple
I	Professional and higher white collar	2.94
II	Lower white collar, commercial	3.38
III	Skilled manual	3.82
IV	Semi-skilled manual	3.79
V	Unskilled	3.88
VI	Textiles	3.31
VII	Coal mining	4.45
VIII	Agricultural laborers	4.57

Table 1. Surviving Children per Married Couple, where Wife's Age Exceeds 45 Years, Classified by Social Status, 1911, England and Wales. Source: England and Wales, Registrar General, *Census of England and Wales*: *1911*, Vol. XIII, "Fertility of Marriage," Part 2 (London: HMSO, 1923), Table 24, pp. 19-20.

Fisher considered the three assumptions made in the above syllogism to be self-evidently true and set about trying to explain why the conditional should also be true, for it is not obvious why those with the greater native endowments and more resources in a society should reproduce less than those with fewer resources and more meagre endowments. Fisher was confronted with the following Darwinian paradox: that in an advanced society the biologically successful are to be found principally among its social failures, while the socially successful are, on the whole, the biological failures (Fisher 1958, pp. 239-240). Nature rarely works this way among other species. Reproductive fitness generally mimics economic or phenotypic fitness.

Fisher believed he had located the cause of this central biological paradox of modern societies in the high inter-class mobility to be found in such societies. As a civilization grows and develops, the elite recruits to itself the most capable and intelligent members of the lower classes. There are, however, two distinct types who take the opportunity of increased social mobility to rise in the social hierarchy. The first are those with high native, i.e., genetic, endowments. The second are those who rise by dint of the low fertility of their parents, as small family size enables such parents to invest proportionately more resources in their children and thereby give them advantages which their colleagues from larger families do not have. The second type, then, rises into the upper classes because of above average environmentally induced endowments rather than above average native talent. Both types interbreed with the "natives" of the upper classes as well as with themselves and with each other. Thus, given a high heritability in fertility, the second type of the upwardly mobile will, through intermarriage with the upper classes, cause a fall in the fertility in these classes, thereby lowering their birth rate and, since the relatively gifted tend to be disproportionately located in the upper classes, also lowering the overall mental endowment of the population as a whole. Over a number of generations, such a process would rob a nation of whatever inheritable, i.e., racial, quality it was that brought it to its preeminence in the first place, presumably produced in the pre-civilization stage (also described by Fisher) where inter-class mobility was low and those with above average native and economic endowments invested such endowments in above average numbers of children, that is, where there was a positive association between social status and number of offspring. Fisher does not tell us why a civilization should require high inter-class mobility to function as such, but we might speculate using the same Darwinian logic employed by Fisher that a form of group selection is operant here, whereby those groups prevail which maximize their genetic potential now (though perhaps in such a way as to lead to the eventual decay of this potential), which maximization can only be done, given the laws of genetic segregation and the consequent irreducible variability in native endowments within classes (Dobzhansky 1973, Cliquet & Delmotte 1981), through substantial transfers of individuals between classes.

In support of this model, Fisher (1958) presented statistical evidence that fertility is highly inheritable, on the order of 40%. That is, 40% of the variation in fertility across women can be attributed to (additive) genetic variation, 60% to environmental, non-genetic variation and non-additive genetic variation. This is a relatively high heritability coefficient and is certainly sufficient to drive the model described above. Later research, however, has failed, after correcting for certain errors in Fisher's method of estimating heritability, to reproduce Fisher's results for his own data as well as for the data of other populations (Williams & Williams 1974). There are in addition strong theoretical reasons for doubting that a high heritability in fertility could exist in any species (Broadhurst, Fulker, & Wilcock 1974). For surely those individuals with higher genetic fecundity would have long ago swamped in numbers those with lower fecundity, thereby extinguishing all genetic variability in this trait across individuals. All recent tests have borne out this prediction (see, for a review, Williams & Williams 1974). There appears to be very little genetic variability in fertility within humans – or within any species (De Fries 1968, p. 326). The more adaptive a trait, the lower its heritability, according to De Fries; and it is difficult to conceive of a trait more adaptive than high fertility.

Where does this leave Fisher's explanation, and the genetic model more generally, of national decay? Contrary to the assertions by some geneticists (e.g., Falconer 1966; Broadhurst, Fulker, & Wilcock 1974), it is left with only minimal damage: it is not necessary that fertility have a high heritability for a differential in the birth rate by social class to exist, and it is the latter which constitutes the essential core of Fisher's model of the deterioration in the human capital of civilized peoples. It is only necessary that this differential exist, for whatever reason, that it persist from generation to generation, that it be a stable feature of civilization. Fisher adduced a high heritability of fertility to explain how the upper classes could under-reproduce without deliberately wishing to do so. It apparently never occurred to him that the more intelligent and the socially and economically advantaged might choose deliberately to suppress their reproduction relative to those less intelligent and with fewer social and economic advantages, for this would run counter to the most fundamental theorem of evolutionary biology, namely, that organisms behave so as to maximize their (relative) reproductive fitness. Some organisms may find themselves in environments where they are forced to restrain their reproduction, but that the greatest restraint occurs in the best environments contradicts this basic theorem. Why there is maximum suppression of fertility among humans in the best environments and with the best endowments is a question I will turn to at the end of this essay. But what needs to be stressed here is that the crucial empirical assumption of Fisher's model is that the upper classes and the more intelligent more generally, under-reproduce relative to the lower classes and the less intelligent and do so persistently, at least in civilized settings. This assumption itself has been recently challenged, however. This is a far more serious challenge to the Fisher model than the finding that fertility has negligible heritability. I describe and evaluate this challenge in the next section.

I.Q., Social Class, and Fertility

Fisher's data, based on census statistics for the most part, showed that birth rates were both lower and falling faster among the upper classes than among the lower classes during the late 19th and early 20th centuries in Great Britain and elsewhere in Europe. Though he had no data on intelligence and fertility, he clearly believed that the negative relationship between social status and fertility implied a negative relationship between intelligence and fertility, too, due to the social promotion of the more able in modern societies, if not in all civilizations. To my knowledge, Fisher's findings and inferences from them were typical of students of differential demography before World War II (see, for a survey of both the research and the data, Wrong 1980). After World War II, the nature of the relationship between I.Q. and fertility was investigated directly by a number of American investigators (Higgins, Reed, & Reed 1962, Bajema 1963, Waller 1971, and Olneck & Wolfe 1980). Interestingly, their findings were universally the reverse of what Fisher and other pre-war investigators anticipated based on their studies of the relationship between social status and fertility. The I.Q./fertility relationship was found to be, if anything, positive. Moreover, the differential birth rate across social and economic classes was also found after the war to be negligible, if not absent altogether, both in the U.S. and in Europe (Kirk 1957, Tabah 1976, Pinnelli 1967).

This finding gave rise to considerable optimism among those concerned, like Fisher, with the apparent prevalence of a dysgenic pattern in birth rates in civilized settings. Frederick Osborn, a leading figure in the American eugenics movement, attributed the novel eugenic trend which emerged after the war to the rise of the modern welfare state, which provided, for the first time, a universal freedom of choice with respect to reproduction, and argued that this trend would be a permanent feature of such states (Osborn & Bajema 1972). He reasoned, not always with translucent logic, that under conditions of freedom of parenthood the more able parents would produce more children. Since such parents, on average, would also be more intelligent, a eugenic trend with respect to intelligence – and with respect to other socially desirable, heritable traits as well – should result. The statistical results were, in fact, altogether a relief for the American eugenics movement, which had nearly been destroyed by its association, at least in name, with German National Socialist eugenic policies (indeed, in retrospect, it can be seen, after the retirement of Osborn, to have *been* destroyed; only his energy and the fortuitous statistical results gave it a semblance of life well into the post-war period). If the welfare state indirectly promoted a eugenic distribution of births, then there would be no reason to call for direct state intervention to produce such a result. The American eugenics movement was thus relieved of having to call for such intervention, which in the post-war climate would have doomed it to a permanent association in many people's minds with the extreme right wing and thereby to permanent residence on the "lunatic fringe" of American politics.

Though the statistical finding of a positive relation between I.Q. and fertility is an altogether sound one, the fact that it had the effect of protecting a vulnerable field of inquiry, i.e., the fields of eugenics and social biology, from being painted with the Nazi tar brush, explains at least in part why this finding has not been replicated and retested on a wider set of samples and time periods (Jensen 1981a). One senses a reluctance in the profession to push this finding too hard, narrow based though it is. As Jensen (1969, 1981a), Cattell (1974), and Osborne (1975) point out, the studies reporting this finding all employed nationally unrepresentative samples (being confined to the native white populations of the Great Lakes states, with the single exception of one of Olneck and Wolf's samples), of cohorts born in the pre-war period, 1910-1940. The narrow base of these samples, in both time and space, has rarely been recognized by the many authors who have cited them as evidence of a eugenic trend with respect to intelligence (Boyd & Richerson 1981, Broadhurst, Fulker, & Wilcock 1974, Eckland 1967, Ehrlich and Feldman 1977, Eysenck 1973, Gottesman 1968, Jencks 1968, Lerner 1968, Lewontin 1970, McClearn 1970, and Weinrich 1978).

In a forthcoming paper (Vining 1982), I show that whereas the positive relationship between social class and fertility as well as between I.Q. and fertility does not appear to be special to the *samples* studied, it does appear to be special to the *age cohort* studied, i.e., the only cohort in modern times to have entered its child-bearing years in a period of rising birth rates. The cohort which produced the so-called baby boom was that born between 1910 and 1940 and reproductively active in the period, 1946-1965, precisely the cohort studied by the several American investigators interested in the I.Q./fertility relationship. Unhappily, Osborn's eugenic hypothesis that welfare states promote a eugenic distribution of births was formulated just before this period (Osborn 1940) and was tested on this cohort alone. In my paper, I examine a national probability sample of the offspring of this cohort, i.e., of men and women born between 1944 and 1954. The latter cohort entered its reproductive years during a much more normal period of falling birth rates. So far, it has exhibited a strong negative relationship between fertility and I.Q. (Table 2) as well as between social status and fertility (U.S. Bureau of the Census 1980), in contrast to the negligible or even positive association between these variables found for its parent cohort. Though the fertility of the younger cohort is not yet complete, it is approaching completion. Moreover, the expected lifetime fertility of this cohort as stated by the cohort itself shows a similar though more moderate negative relationship (Table 3, U.S. Bureau of the Census 1980). The ultimate slope of the relationship between I.Q. and fertility will probably fall somewhere in between that found for current cumulative fertility and that found for expected lifetime fertility, as women with below average fertility tend to overestimate their lifetime fertility, and women with above average fertility to underestimate it. One would also expect that the less intelligent would have more children than they expect because of a greater failure rate in contraception (Udry 1978, Cliquet & Balcaen 1979), whereas the more intelligent would have fewer children than they anticipate due to lower fecundity in the later childbearing years as well as unexpected demands of outside-the-home careers in which the more intelligent would be disproportionately represented (Bajema 1978).

Ignoring mortality differentials across I.Q. classes, which are probably small, at least for women, and ignoring generation length differentials, which are small in effect when fertility is near replacement levels, as it is, and assuming a heritability in I.Q. of 0.5, the best estimate of the overall generational shift in mean I.Q. due to fertility differentials in this cohort is approximately 1 I.Q. point per generation (Vining 1982). If this magnitude of generational change in average levels of intelligence were typical of modern nations undergoing the demographic transition, then a population could conceivably experience a significant decline in the mean level of mental ability over the period of this transition – and even beyond if one anticipates, as seems reasonable, that in periods of low, constant fertility as well, those of higher intelligence are both more inclined and more able to suppress reproduction. For approximately 180 years or five to six generations have passed since birth rates began to fall in the U.S. (see Figure 1 below) and Great Britain (Smith 1981, p. 597). Only the baby boom

TABLE 2. Mean Cumulative Fertility Rate According to Measured Intelligence of Parent Generation, Probability Sample of U.S. Population, Aged 25-34, 1976 (white men) and 1978 (women).

Sub-Group	I.Q. Range						
	≤ 70	71-85	86-100	101-115	116-130	> 130	All
White women (estimated standard error)	1.59(.32)	1.68(.11)	1.76(.06)	1.44(.04)	1.15(.06)	0.92(.17)	1.46(.03)
(Sample Size)	(17)	(122)	(522)	(907)	(438)	(60)	(2066)
Black women (estimated standard error)	2.60(.22)	2.12(.13)	1.79(.11)	1.63(.14)	1.20(.53)	0.00(---)	1.94(.07)
(Sample Size)	(50)	(165)	(159)	(88)	(10)	(1)	(473)
White men (estimated standard error)	1.17(.25)	1.30(.11)	1.29(.05)	1.19(.04)	0.84(.06)	0.45(.11)	1.14(.03)
(Sample Size)	(24)	(142)	(565)	(825)	(377)	(60)	(1993)

Source: Vining (1982)

Note: Black men are omitted due to deficiencies in the basic data.

TABLE 3. Mean Expected Lifetime Fertility, According to Measured Intelligence of Parent Generation, Probability Sample of U.S. Women, Aged 25-34, 1978.

Sub-Group	I.Q. Range						
	≤ 70	71-85	86-100	101-115	116-130	> 130	All
White Women	2.31	2.16	2.30	2.14	2.03	1.93	2.15
(estimated standard error)	(.38)	(.11)	(.06)	(.04)	(.06)	(.18)	(.03)
Sample Size	16	122	517	893	432	59	2039
Black Women	3.20	2.75	2.36	2.25	2.30	2.00	2.56
(estimated standard error)	(.26)	(.13)	(.11)	(.15)	(.47)	(---)	(.07)
Sample Size	50	161	155	88	10	1	465

Source: Vining (1982)

Note: Data on expected lifetime fertility unavailable for men.

TABLE 4. Mean Number of Children Ever Born By Wife's Education and Husband's Education for Japan and Selected Western Countries.

Country	Education of Wife					Education of Husband				
	Less Than Elementary	Elementary	Lower Secondary	Higher Secondary	Post Secondary	Less Than Elementary	Elementary	Lower Secondary	Higher Secondary	Post Secondary
Japan (1977)	1.89			1.81	1.69	1.89			1.81	1.75
Belgium (1966)	3.12	2.09	2.00	1.95	2.07	2.73	2.07	1.94	2.17	2.07
Czechoslovakia (1970)	2.27		1.64		1.64	2.21		1.71		1.64
Denmark (1970)	2.12		1.80	1.83	1.89	2.11		1.85	1.87	1.79
England & Wales (1967)	1.86		1.73		1.69	1.85		1.70		1.72
Finland (1971)	2.68	2.18	1.60		1.86	2.33	2.07	1.92		1.80
France (1972)	4.25	2.28	1.92	1.92	1.89	3.91	2.28	1.97	1.92	2.08
Hungary (1966)	3.24	2.19	1.72	1.46	1.34	3.07	2.17	1.75	1.43	1.50
Poland (1972)	2.89	2.85	2.33	1.82	1.60	2.82	2.84	2.40	1.94	1.60
U.S.A. (1970)	2.94		2.67	2.24	2.05	2.87		2.50	2.27	2.12
Yugoslavia (1970)	2.78	2.03	1.82	1.43	1.34	3.09	2.28	2.01	1.69	1.55

Source: Nohara-Atoh (1980, p. 114).

Note: Average standardized by duration of marriage.

TABLE 5. Average number of children for men listed in WHO'S WHO 1980-81, by age, with comparable data for United States women.

Cohorts Born	Age in 1979	Men in WHO'S WHO 1980-81		Cumulative Birth Rates to White Women as of January 1, 1979
		Number of Men	Average No. of Children (estimated standard error)	
before 1900	80 and over	96	1.84 (.15)	
1900-1904	75-79	131	2.01 (.11)	2.44
1905-1909	70-74	248	2.30 (.09)	2.27
1910-1914	65-69	467	2.41 (.07)	2.28
1915-1919	60-64	544	2.55 (.07)	2.48
1920-1924	55-59	655	2.73 (.06)	2.75
1925-1929	50-54	624	2.95 (.06)	2.95
1930-1934	45-49	435	2.57 (.07)	3.10
1935-1939	40-44	275	2.30 (.08)	2.92
1940-1944	35-39	112	1.92 (.13)	2.43
1945 and later	Under 35	51	1.10 (.19)	
TOTAL		3638	2.52	

Source: Vining (1983).

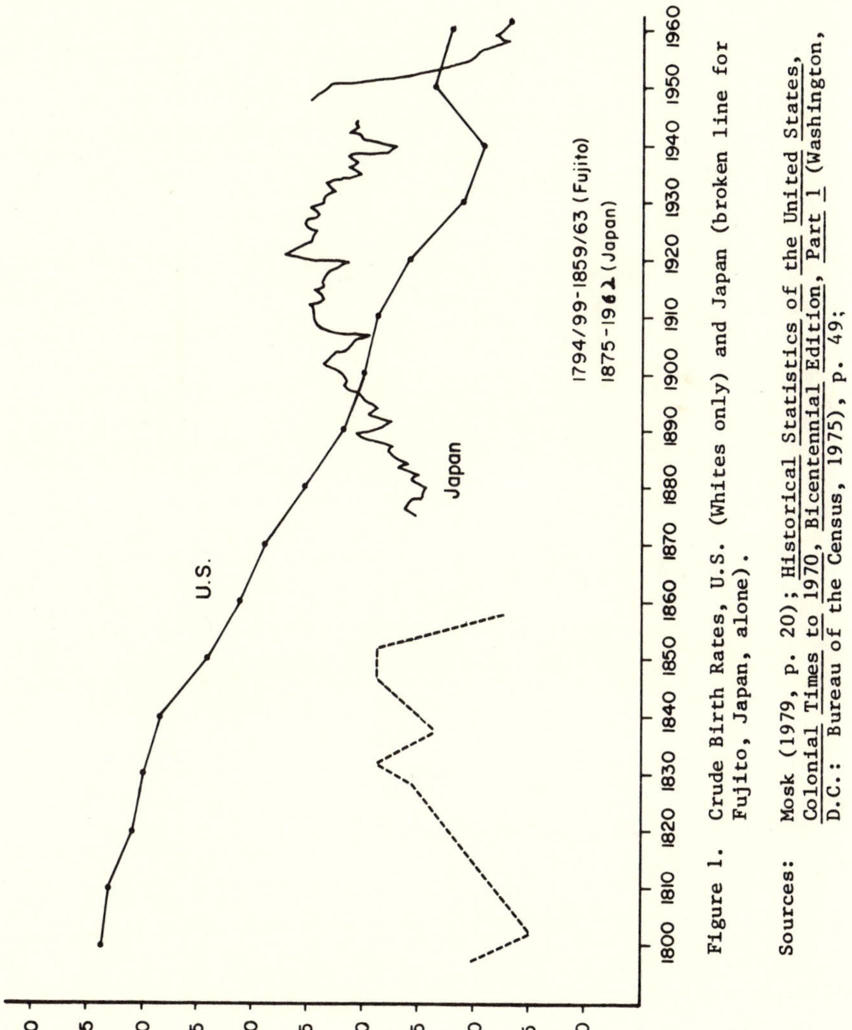

Figure 1. Crude Birth Rates, U.S. (Whites only) and Japan (broken line for Fujito, Japan, alone).

Sources: Mosk (1979, p. 20); Historical Statistics of the United States, Colonial Times to 1970, Bicentennial Edition, Part 1 (Washington, D.C.: Bureau of the Census, 1975), p. 49;

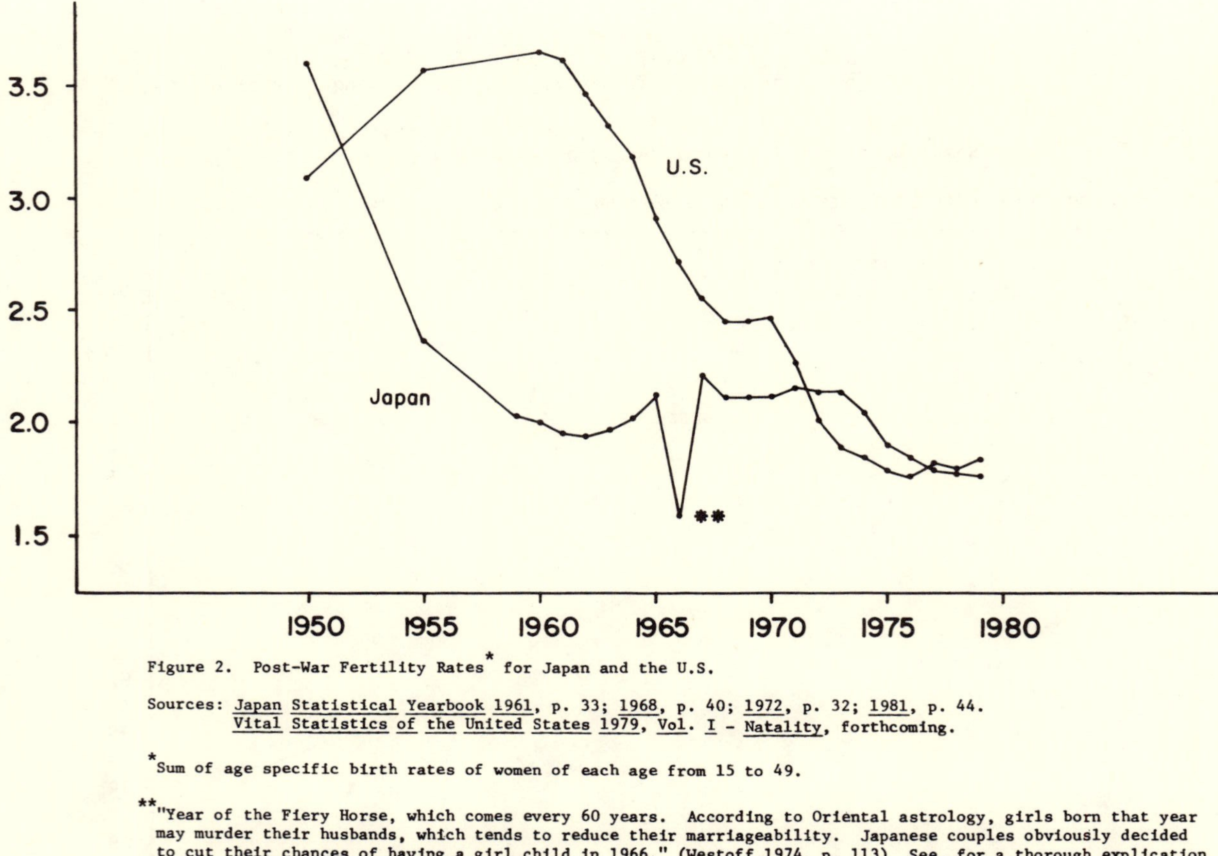

Figure 2. Post-War Fertility Rates* for Japan and the U.S.

Sources: Japan Statistical Yearbook 1961, p. 33; 1968, p. 40; 1972, p. 32; 1981, p. 44. Vital Statistics of the United States 1979, Vol. I - Natality, forthcoming.

*Sum of age specific birth rates of women of each age from 15 to 49.

**"Year of the Fiery Horse, which comes every 60 years. According to Oriental astrology, girls born that year may murder their husbands, which tends to reduce their marriageability. Japanese couples obviously decided to cut their chances of having a girl child in 1966." (Westoff 1974, p. 113) See, for a thorough explication of this phenomenon, Aymans (1980).

years and an earlier 20 year period of rising birth rates in Great Britain in the mid-19th century (Smith 1981, p. 597), reversed the presumably dysgenic trend attendant upon this decline. Thus, one might predict, using some admittedly heroic extrapolations from current data (though there is no reason to believe the severity of the dysgenic trend to have been any lower in the past than now) a four to five point drop in mean I.Q. to have accompanied the demographic transition in Great Britain and the U.S.(1) A drop of this magnitude could have the effect on the national character claimed for it by Fisher. As is pointed out by Huxley (1963), and is well known to students of differential demography, even small changes in the mean of a normal distribution, which characterizes most biological traits including that measured by I.Q., can cause quite dramatic shifts in the relative frequencies in the respective tails of the distribution. For example, a decline in mean I.Q. of 5 points will reduce the number of persons with I.Q.'s over 130 (if the original mean were at 100) by almost 60%. If the civilization in question were dependent upon the existence of this highly able group, then obviously a decline of this magnitude in its relative size could have the kind of impact which Fisher postulated.

Note here that nothing about the heritability of fertility need be assumed in making the kind of extrapolations made above – only that, for whatever reason (but reasons I speculate upon in the last section of this paper), the population in question replicates generation after generation a dysgenic pattern of births. I also assume here, with Fisher, a high heritability in I.Q. – or at least that the parent-child correlation in I.Q. is strongly positive. The latter fact is indisputable. Whether this high correlation is due to genetic inheritance or early family culture is a matter of dispute, though the most parsimonious, indeed the only, model of the observed mathematical pattern of correlations between relatives of different degrees is the simple polygenic one (Bouchard & McGue 1981). But unlike fertility, no one disputes that the trait measured by I.Q. is passed on in some manner from parent to child, either through the genes or

(1) Wrong (1980, p. 48) states that class differentials in fertility rates in the West most probably emerged several generations before the decline in aggregate fertility that began in the 19th century. Thus, the estimate made here of the number of generations having a dysgenic pattern of births may very well be an under-estimate.

through early family culture. Indeed, as Corning (1972, p. 261) has argued:

> "the heritability issue may not even be germane. If there are strong parent-offspring correlations with respect to various behavioral traits, it may not be particularly important whether or not these correlations are the result of genetic transmission or family culture or both ..." (see, on this same point, Jensen 1981b).

Of course, I am not claiming here that other forces could not or will not move the mean I.Q. in the other direction. The large decline in mean S.A.T. scores in the United States observed since the middle 1960s (Zajonc & Bargh 1980) ironically happened to the baby-boom cohort, a cohort which, according to all evidence, was born during a rare eugenic period (though the trend in I.Q. scores for the baby boom cohort is more ambiguous, see Thorndike 1977, Roberts 1971, and Berger 1978, p. 30). By contrast, the cohorts born in the 1920s and 1930s during a period of supposedly dysgenic trends have shown unambiguous increases in both mean I.Q. and mean S.A.T. scores (Duncan 1952, Zajonc 1976). Neither the size nor the direction of these large swings over time in mean scores on intelligence and aptitude tests in the U.S. can be explained (contrary to a statement in Karlsson's recent treatise on the genetics of intelligence and creativity, Karlsson 1978, p. 187) as lagged expressions of previous swings in the fertility/intelligence relationship. As such, they suggest a greater empirical influence of certain cultural and educational movements on the central tendency of a population's intelligence, particularly in adolescence, than the hereditarians have been inclined to concede. Still, the unwillingness on the part of a large number of highly intelligent and successful persons to replace themselves such as we seem to be observing today in the U.S., cannot help, given the widely acknowledged high correlation between intelligence of parent and child, but have an influence on the character of the next generation, perhaps simply by lowering the mean around which these educational and cultural innovations cause the measured central tendency of intelligence to fluctuate. A particularly vulnerable time for a civilization might be a period when a dysgenic reproductive pattern is reinforced rather than counteracted by such innovations. The West may be entering such a period now.

There are, of course, other traits, including mental ones,

which are important to advanced civilization and which are probably not captured by the I.Q. test (though insofar as they are measurable quantitatively they may be highly intercorrelated with I.Q. – Cattell (1972, p. 378) says, however, that now the correlations approach zero): conscientiousness, altruism, steadfastness, courage, sympathy, creativity, inventiveness, integrity of character, aesthetic discrimination. Most such traits like I.Q. probably have either high heritabilities or at least high parent-child correlations, due to genetic transmission or to family culture in the early years of child-rearing, that is, before the wider society begins to educate and mold the child. Thus, a positive research strategy for critics of the I.Q. measure and its almost exclusive use in studies of eugenic or dysgenic trends would be to test either directly or indirectly for a eugenic pattern of births with respect to these other traits as well. There is no reason that I know of to believe that persons well endowed with these unmeasured mental and character traits are not suppressing their fertility at a rate equal to that observed for high I.Q. persons. Indeed, there is every reason to believe that the blandishments of the ZPG movement have had greatest effect on this class of people (Weyl 1973). However, there is no hard evidence to back up such impressions, to my knowledge.

At the same time, most students of the subject acknowledge that the I.Q. test certainly measures a cognitive trait important to a modern economy, though perhaps not all-important. There is no better evidence of this fact than the very high published mean I.Q. of that population empirically observed to be best fit for life and work in such an economy, that is, for the maintenance and running of the very complex systems which go under the rubric of the modern economy, i.e., the population of Japan. The very high measured mean I.Q. and the very high economic productivity of the Japanese cannot be coincidental. (2)

(2) Seventy years ago, Veblen noted the "facile apprehension of Occidental methods and values in the domain of material knowledge" among the Japanese, as compared to the seeming inability among other peoples, "even under hard compulsion," to "effect anything like a practicable working arrangement with the Occidental system of mechanical efficiency and economic control" (Veblen 1915a, p. 31). Though he accepted as a matter of fact the racial [i.e., genetic] origin of national differences (Arrow 1975), Veblen appeared not to subscribe to the genetic model of national decay, at least as applied to modern nations, preferring to see such decay as due to the inevitable institutional deterioration brought on by the corrosive effects

The Gap in Average Intelligence Levels between Japan and the West

Richard Lynn has published three articles with estimates of the mean Japanese I.Q., all of which show it to exceed that of Great Britain as well as of white Americans by 3-11 I.Q. points; the best estimate for the post-war cohort born in the middle 1960s is at the upper side of this range (Lynn 1977, 1982; Lynn & Dziobon 1980). Lynn speculates that the lower mean I.Q. of the pre-war birth cohort may be due to the poor diet and other kinds of physical deprivation experienced by this cohort during the war and immediate post-war period. The cohort born in the 1960s, by contrast, has been raised in an environment materially not too different from that prevalent in Europe and the U.S.

Nathaniel Weyl, however, has expressed skepticism concerning the size (though not the sign) of the Japan-U.S. difference in mean I.Q. (see also the remarks in Cattell & Brennan 1981). (3) For, as he says, a 10% superiority in arithmetic mean "would presuppose such a decisive Nipponese superiority at the highest intelligence levels as to give Japan leadership in all fields of creative intellectual endeavor." (Weyl 1978, p. 70) A ten point gap in mean I.Q., given that the standard deviations of both distributions are equal to 15, implies 4 times as many persons with I.Q.'s over 130 (where the lower mean is 100) and 14 times as many persons with I.Q.'s over 160. Indeed, even a three point gap implies a still significant, though more moderate, superiority of 58% and 120% in these two classes. But whereas the Japanese have achieved superiority in industrial production, they appear not to have achieved superiority or even parity in creative intellectual endeavor, at least not yet. As Ellsworth Huntington reported over 70 years ago, "The Japanese are generally conceded to be remarkable for a high average of mental development rather than for individuals of exceptional brilliancy." (Huntington 1912, p. 260) A recent article in the Sunday Business Section of *The New York Times* presents essentially the same thesis (Lohr 1982).

of capitalism on certain precapitalist habits and classes which were essential to the efficiency of that very capitalism (Veblen 1915a, 1915b). I shall review this successional model of national decay, which assumes a constancy in the genetic constitution of the population in question, in a subsequent paper.

(3) There are also reports that the gap discovered by Lynn has not been replicated by other psychologists using different cognitive tests (Garmon 1982), but the results of this research have yet to be published.

A number of possible explanations suggest themselves to account for the paradox posed by Weyl. For example, in making the above illustrative calculations, I assumed equal variances in the I.Q. distributions of the West and Japan, but there is good reason to hypothesize that the Japanese variance is lower (or that the Japanese distribution has less kurtosis, i.e., is thinner-tailed). Freedman (1979) speculates that the Japanese population is significantly more homozygous than the contemporary populations of the U.S. and Great Britain. According to Freedman (1979), the Japanese have been genetically isolated since 300 A.D. No large-scale military invasions or folk migrations have taken place from the Asian mainland since that time. There is no population of this size in the world, according to Freedman, which has been genetically isolated for anywhere near the number of generations the Japanese have. Britain, comprising the small group of islands at the other end of the Eurasian continent, was invaded by successive waves, between 400 A.D. and 900 A.D., of Saxons, Angles, Danes and Norsemen and by smaller but possibly reproductively important numbers of Normans after 1066. It has failed to maintain genetic isolation into modern times as the Japanese have done. In the modern period, there has been considerable migration into Britain of Huguenots and Jews, not to speak of the steady influx of diverse genetic elements over the past two hundred years as a result of worldwide colonial adventures and the substantial post-war immigration of Pakistanis and East and West Indians. Of course, no more heterogenous and heterozygous population exists than that of the U.S.A.

In Japan, by contrast, 600,000 Japanese-Koreans constitute the only notable minority; and it is significant that although many of these are of second or third generation, they are far from being assimilated – despite their being virtually indistinguishable from the Japanese, and their small numbers. Japanese-born Koreans who speak only Japanese must still apply for citizenship upon reaching their majority, and they are by no means assured of a successful application (Lee 1981). In no other country of the world is ethnicity so determinant of nationality. In fact, there is even reported to be some reluctance by the Japanese authorities to allow the opening up of any more imperial tombs to study further the origins of the Japanese people, as the results might bring the date of Japanese isolation closer to 300-400 A.D. than to the traditional 660

B.C. and thereby the origins of the Japanese themselves much closer to those of the Koreans (De Vos & Lee 1981, p.7). Freedman (1979) speculates that the very high degree of altruism, cooperativeness, and social cohesion observed in the Japanese population is due to the high degree of genetic relatedness of this population, large though it is. Certainly, the Japanese themselves place great importance upon their homogeneity and long genetic isolation, as is shown by their treatment of even very closely related minorities, such as the Japanese-Koreans, and their reported reluctance to pursue the scientific study of their origins with all the vigor for which they are so well known.

One implication of the greater genetic homogeneity of the Japanese is that polygenic quantitative traits there should, on this hypothesis, show lower dispersion around their means. I am aware of no published evidence on this question, though it would certainly seem possible to use the same data used by Lynn to test this hypothesis for the Japanese I.Q. distribution. National data on morphological traits ought likewise to be available to test Freedman's hypothesis. (4)

A second possible explanation for Weyl's paradox is the fact that high intelligence is only a necessary condition for creativity, not a sufficient one (Jensen 1980). There is at least anecdotal evidence that the Japanese educational system acts to suppress the development of creative habits of mind. Deviance of thought, which is at the heart of creativity, would on this hypothesis

(4) Freedman's hypothesis of a greater homozygosity in the Japanese population is put forward here as just that – a hypothesis. There is a long-standing hypothesis to the contrary. Veblen (1915a), for example, describes the Japanese as a hybrid population like that of the West, and Coon (1965, p. 134) remarks that "Japan was an archaeologically variable and busy region in late Pleistocene and early post-Pleistocene times," being the destination of several diverse peoples. Despite the unusually long period of Japanese isolation stressed by Freedman, it is conceivable that a caste-like organization could have prevented the intermingling of the descendants of these various diverse elements in the Japanese population. The Eta, of course, are a well-known, largely unassimilated lower caste group in Japan, numbering about 2 million (De Vos and Wagatsuma 1966). Less well known are the descendants of Samurai, formerly themselves a caste-like group and also numbering about 2 million, who occupy today a disproportionate number of the higher positions in education, government, and business (Yasuda 1969), and may very well be continuing to inter-marry to a considerable degree. Whether these relatively endogamous elements are the descendants of different pre-historic migrant populations in Japan is, as far as I know, an unanswered and perhaps even an unresearched question. I am not competent to comment further on this counter-hypothesis to that of Freedman, who obviously assumes something approximating panmixia in Japan.

be particularly absent from the Japanese elite, which has been selected almost exclusively on the basis of their academic performance in an extremely demanding and rigid educational system which hardly varies across the whole of Japan. Admission into the elite national universities is based solely on achievement tests on specific academic subjects. A capacity for hard work, high intelligence, great attention to detail are what promotes one in such a system – but certainly not an ability to think outside of established frameworks, which is the mark of the creative mind. In fact, creative habits could only act as a drag on one's performance in such a system.

However, it is possible that it is not the Japanese educational system that is the true independent variable here, but rather the character of the Japanese people which that educational system was unconsciously designed to fit. For the relative absence of inventiveness among the Japanese appears to predate the Meiji era, when the current educational system was put into place. Befu (1971) informs us that Japan "has always been at a periphery of major cultural centers, ... where most cultural innovations occur and from which these innovations diffuse. Historical and geographical circumstances have made Japan principally a borrower or receiver of cultural innovations ... [T]here are very few basic inventions which can be attributed to the Japanese ... Rather, Japan has expended its energy in integrating what it borrows with the indigenous culture. Japan's uniqueness ... lies in its ability to work out 'stylistic' refinements of borrowed elements." (Befu 1971, p. 33) To what extent the culture molded by the historical and geographical circumstances of the Japanese also exerted selective pressure on genes controlling certain behavioral traits, the high frequency of which in turn molded the culture, is unknown. Lumsden and Wilson (1981) show that – in theory at least – it is possible for significant genetic changes to occur in response to a stable cultural pattern in a thousand years – their so-called "thousand-year rule". Freedman (1979) shows convincingly that certain neonatal traits of the Mongoloid, such as docility and relatively low proneness towards irritability, are genetic in origin. Unfortunately, there has been no sociobiological research on the Japanese *per se*.(5)

(5) There is apparently almost a complete lack of interest by the Japanese in sociobiology, at least as applied to humans, as well as in I.Q. studies and genetic

What is of immediate interest, however, is the rather large gap in the locations (i.e., central tendencies) of the distributions of cognitive ability in Japan and the West. For it is the high average level of intelligence among the Japanese which accounts (at least in part) for their success – indeed, preeminence – in many areas of industrial and advanced economic activity, though it must be granted that so far they have shown relatively little aptitude for (or interest in) thinking about the institutional framework which nurtures this activity or for contributing the basic innovations which drive it. Theirs is an unexcelled ability – in the language of economists – "to maximize an objective funtion" in a game whose rules have been invented elsewhere. An ability to become self-conscious about the game itself, whose rules must be continually changed if it is to be improved or even survive, has not yet shown itself among the Japanese. But here we merely seek the origins of their very great playing ability. Japanese demography has several distinct characteristics, in addition to those of genetic demography speculated upon above, which may provide some clues to these origins.

Demographic Differences between Japan and the West

The demography of modern Japan has three characteristics which distinguish it from that of the West. 1) In Japan, there was not the one or two century-long gradual decline in fertility which we observe in the West, but rather a very abrupt fall in fertility, in the early 1950s, from a nearly constant and quite high level of fertility which had persisted as far back as the

models of variations in human intelligence. Cummings (1980) remarks that "Japanese scholars, who are such vigorous translators of American fad books, have shown almost no interest in the currently popular American books that examine the heredity-intelligence-school achievement link." According to Cummings, "Japanese educators have never paid much attention to the innate abilities of learners. They have tended to assume that anybody can learn a task given a determined effort ... Japan's high opinion of effort is complemented by a relative disinterest in heredity ..." (p. 151) In an earlier paper, Cummings (1977) attributes the absence of I.Q. studies in Japan to political resistance from the socialist teachers' union, as well as from the right. Atsuhiro (1980) notes a "near-absence of sociobiology in Japan" (p. 262). Freedman's (1979) discussion of Japan provides one clue as to the origins of this disinterest, namely, the possibility that natural selection there has exhausted a much larger part of the heritable variability in the population (see n. 7 below) than it has had the opportunity to in more open populations, such as those of Great Britain and the U.S.

data on Japanese fertility go (Mosk 1979, see Figure 1). 2) Fertility differentials by social and economic class and by educational attainment are negligible in Japan, in contrast in particular to the U.S. where the distribution of per-capita births across the different educational and income classes is far from being uniform and where the poor and the less educated bear a disproportionate number of the nation's children (Nohara-Atoh 1980, 1981a; see, for data on fertility differentials by education attainment, Table 4).(6) 3) Since its abrupt fall in the early 1950s, Japanese fertility has remained at a remarkably constant, slightly above replacement, level, at least until recently, in contrast again to the U.S. in particular, where there have been substantial fluctuations in fertility over the post-war period (Figure 2). In short, Japanese fertility has been marked by abrupt, rather than smooth, transitions, between which stretch long periods of relative stability.

(6) Table 4 actually shows comparably negligible differentials in most West European countries (i.e., Belgium, Denmark, France, Great Britain), after removing the numerically insignificant (though potentially reproductively significant, Cliquet & Balcaen 1979) class of persons with less than an elementary education. It is in East Europe and the U.S. where the differentials are large. Note, however, that Nohara-Atoh's data for countries other than Japan are for the cohort reproductively active in the 1960s whereas for Japan his data are for the 1970s. The 1960s were a period of generally high fertility in West Europe when one might expect narrow fertility differentials by educational attainment. The 1970s, by contrast, should reveal much wider differentials, being a period of rapid fertility reduction which, according to casual observation, appears to be particularly marked among the educated. Unfortunately, no data on fertility differentials in Europe during the 1970s are available, except for a brief report on the distribution of *legitimate* live births in England and Wales in the *Eugenics Society Bulletin* (Anon. 1981). Note also that Nohara-Atoh's data are confined to marital fertility. Such data exclude from the numerator of the ratio between births and population at risk, most illegitimate births, and from the denominator, unmarried persons. Illegitimate births, while negligible in Japan, constitute a significant percentage of all births in many countries of the West (United Nations 1976, Table 32) and are probably concentrated among the less educated. Though in previous generations, the exclusion of unmarried persons would have biased the distribution of per-capita births by educational attainment in a dysgenic direction, because of a lower marriage rate among the less intelligent (Higgins, Reed, & Reed 1962), it is less clear what the direction and degree of bias is for the current generation of men and women of reproductive ages in either Japan or the West. In the absence of any other information, perhaps the best assumption is that the degree and direction of bias is the same in both. Under this assumption, Nohara-Atoh's data significantly understate the difference in fertility differentials between Japan and the West, because of the exclusion of illegitimate births from the data of the latter. His data are the only comparative data on fertility differentials available, to my knowledge, however. We badly need both a comparative study of current fertility differentials, which avoids the defects of Nohara-Atoh's, and a study of historical fertility differentials in Japan, which we lack altogether.

There is a theorem in demography that fertility differentials increase during periods of overall fertility decline (O'Connell 1981, p. 12). By this theorem, one would expect Japan to have experienced less pronounced fertility differentials because periods of fertility decline have been rather infrequent there. In the West, by contrast, the periods of decline in fertility have been long and drawn out and, thus, according to this theorem, the fertility differentials by class should have been more pronounced there.

It is interesting in this respect that Japan alone among the developed countries has an explicitly eugenic law at the national level. Though this law has primarily served, in the face of severe population pressures in the immediate post-war period caused by the repatriation of Japanese colonists and a very high birth rate, to promote a lower rate of growth in the Japanese population as a whole, through an easing of restrictions on abortions, framers of the Japanese Eugenics Law explicitly recognized the danger of fertility suppression being concentrated among certain classes and types of individuals and, at least at the beginning, monitored the effects of the law to see if any such differential pattern was emerging.(7) A report by a Cabinet Population Problem Council stated, "If conception control is practiced only among a part of the well-educated class, it is feared that the quality of the people will be lowered. It should be evenly

(7) The Japanese geneticist, Ei Matsunaga, states flatly that "no eugenics movement has ever existed in [Japan] " (Matsunaga 1968, p. 199), but this is, strictly speaking, a misrepresentation of history. The *Eugenics Review* (1931) reports the establishment of a "Japanese Society of Race Hygiene at the Physiological Institute of the Imperial University of Tokyo," and Steiner (1938) notes "the rise in a new interest in problems of population quality" in Japan as "seen in the recent establishment of a Society for the Promotion of Hygienic Marriages" (p. 723). Nisot's exhaustive review of national eugenics movements also documents the existence of a "Eugenics Society of Japan" (Nisot 1929, p. 344). And we have just seen that there was definitely an interest on the part of the Japanese government in the eugenics problem in the immediate post-war period, though apparently no eugenics movement *per se*. It is possible that the pre-war organizations were simply deferential replicas, lacking any real roots in Japanese intellectual and scientific culture, of counterparts in the other Axis nations, where the interest in eugenics was evidently a very broad and deep one, so that Matsunaga's statement, while technically in error, does convey the correct impression. However, there was an earlier eugenics movement of indisputably indigenous origins described by Yanaga (1949, p. 97) which had as its goal the intermarriage of Japanese with Caucasians so as to improve the racial stock of the former. According to Yanaga, this, to the modern sensibility, rather bizarre idea was discussed and debated in the highest government circles during the 1880s. Whereas for Yanaga this movement demonstrates how all-pervasive the feeling of inferiority towards Westerners was in Japan, for our purposes here it simply demonstrates a

disseminated to every bracket of society both in urban and rural areas and in every educational and occupational group" (quoted in Whelpton 1949, p. 45; see also Koya 1957). Thus, as the abrupt decline in fertility in Japan in the early 1950s has all the marks of being by design (Mosk 1979, p. 37), so too does its uniform expression across classes, groups, and regions. The slow diffusion of fertility decline from the upper classes downward and from the cities outwards, which is characteristic of the West, does not seem to have been as prominent a feature of the demographic transition in Japan (see, concerning regional variations in fertility in Japan, Tsubouchi 1970).

It is possible now to at least hypothesize a link between these differences in aggregate and differential demography between Japan and the West and the gap in the overall level of intelligence which appears to have opened up between the two. My own data on the magnitude of the dysgenic trend now current in the U.S is roughly consistent with this hypothesis. If we assume that the overall intelligence levels of the Japanese and Western peoples were approximately the same at the beginning of the 19th century, then the subsequent 180 years would have been sufficient, given a 1 point decline in mean I.Q. per generation in the West and a stable mean in Japan, to create a not insignificant part of the gap now observed. That is to say, Japan effected its demographic transition very largely in the space of a couple of years and monitored it carefully to make sure that it had no dysgenic consequences. The West, by contrast, experienced a slow, laissez-faire demographic transition in which fertility decline diffused downwards from the upper classes and which, if we may extrapolate from my own data on

capacity for eugenic reasoning and an interest in eugenic solutions to social problems (in this case, Japan's backwardness relative to the West) on the part of the Japanese, a capacity and interest whose origins were quite probably independent of similar tendencies in the West. The lack of any *current* interest in the subject of eugenics on the part of the Japanese may be simply because it is irrelevant to them, at least as long as miscegenation is ruled out. As Freedman (1979) suggests, natural selection may have exhausted a large part of the heritable variability *within* the Japanese population. This hypothesis implies a low heritability in such traits as intelligence among the Japanese and probably a low variance in their phenotypic expression as well, since environmental variance is not likely to be high in so culturally homogenous and highly centralized a nation. Both of these implications of Freedman's theory are testable, but, to my knowledge, neither has been tested. Alternatively, the current lack of interest in eugenics in Japan may be simply because the political climate is not hospitable to hereditarian ideas (Cummings 1977), given their association with the defeat and the failures of Japan's militarist and imperialist era.

I.Q. and fertility for the U.S. and from studies of differential fertility by income and social class for the pre-war generations, had significant dysgenic consequences for its population. Though only speculative, this hypothesis surely deserves further study, as it ties together a number of disparate phenomena that have hitherto been isolated.

A Sociobiological Model of Dysgenic Fertility

I return now to the problem of explaining the pattern of differential and dysgenic fertility in the West (as well as the absence of this pattern in Japan). Recall that Fisher's hypothesis of a progressive sterilization of the upper classes (who recruit the more able in any given generation) was found faulty on at least three grounds. 1) The upper classes have shown themselves, most notably during the baby-boom, capable of raising their fertility to and even above the national average. For example, cohorts of men in the American *Who's Who* born between 1905 and 1930 exhibit fertility rates slightly exceeding those of the same cohorts of white women in the U.S. as a whole (Table 5, see also Sly and Richards 1972). Under Fisher's hypothesis that the upper classes suffer from progressively lower fecundity, such sudden lurches upward in their fertility should be difficult, if not impossible. 2) The heritability of fertility, which has to be high for Fisher's model to work, has been shown repeatedly by subsequent investigators to be near zero. 3) Finally, the fertility of the upwardly mobile, which by Fisher's model should be lower than average, has been shown by at least some measures and for some cohorts to be higher than average (Stevens 1981). In short, below average fertility among members of the upper classes, among the more intelligent and among those with more resources more generally, appears to be deliberate in the West. Contrary to Fisher's model, low fertility did not creep up on the upper classes through intermarriage with upwardly mobile but infertile members of the lower classes. The paradox observed in the West of low biological fitness among those socially and economically fit still presents human sociobiology with one of its most challenging problems.

The most exhaustive and imaginative recent attack on this problem is that of Barkow & Burley (1980) and Burley (1979). Intelligence, argue Barkow and Burley, obviously conferred upon its possessors tremendous selective advantages. In no other way are we able to explain the explosive growth of the hominid brain in the past million years (Godfrry & Jacobs 1981). "No other organ in the history of life has grown faster." (Wilson 1978, p. 87) At the same time, this enhancement of intelligence increased the females' appreciation of and foresight with respect to the dangers, pains, and inconvenience of child birth and child rearing and thereby her will as well as her ability to control her fertility, thus potentially threatening her fitness. As a consequence, other traits, both cultural and innate, evolved to counter the one great selective *dis*advantage of intelligence, namely, that it would cause its possessors, particularly females, to under-reproduce. Examples of such traits are concealed ovulation (unique to the human), continuous sexual receptivity and strong sexual desire ("[h]uman beings are unique among the primates in the intensity and variety of their sexual activity" (Wilson 1978, p. 140)), male dominance, and pro-natalist dogmas and ideologies. "With the growth of intelligence," write Barkow and Burley, "early hominid females eventually understood the relationship between ovulation, copulation, and fertilization. They used this new knowledge to control their fertility, reducing it to the point of eliminating their genes from the gene-pool. Since intelligence itself was of high adaptive value, selection reduced not female intelligence but awareness of ovulation." The universality of pro-natalist dogmas likewise suggests a reluctance on the part of females to bear children. "Why should so many societies both pressure and reward women for childbearing, if women were not reluctant to have children . . . ?" Barkow and Burley rhetorically ask. In fact, a whole complex of genetic and cultural traits, which Barkow and Burley describe, evolved to prevent women from using their intelligence to suppress their reproduction.

The modern economy, however, typically provides women with both the autonomy (e.g., freedom from male dominance, equal opportunity for employment in the money economy) and the means (e.g., efficient and safe methods of contraception) to thwart the various devices which had evolved, in turn, to thwart the human female's predisposition to under-reproduce. (Why modernization has this effect is another question which is not addressed by Burley and Barkow and which lies well beyond the scope of this paper.) Furthermore, the higher the intelligence of the woman in the modern setting, the greater her access to situations in society which will allow her the autonomy she requires to be able to suppress reproduction as well as the greater the foresight of the pains and inconvenience of child birth and child-rearing and hence the greater the will to use the contraceptive devices which modernization provides her to avoid reproduction. Sex, in which both the human male and the female have an exceptional interest relative to other mammals (Wilson 1978), can likewise be enjoyed by the more intelligent in the modern setting without the consequences of child-bearing, though Kinsey reported the more educated to be less sexually active as well (Haldane 1956). In short, despite its overall adaptive value, intelligence leads in the modern setting to maladaptive behavior.(8)

Barkow and Burley remark that this maladaptive behavior should be highly adaptive at the level of the species (though for

(8) That luxury promotes a certain reproductive laziness and other kinds of biological and cultural deterioration among humans is an hypothesis as old as the ancients. Polybius: "In our time all Greece was visited by a dearth of children and generally a decay of population ... this evil grew upon us rapidly, and without attracting attention, by our men becoming perverted to a passion for show and money and the pleasures of an idle life, and accordingly either not marrying at all, or, if they did marry, refusing to rear the children that were born, or at most one or two out of a great number, for the sake of leaving them well off or bringing them up in extravagant luxury." (Shuckburg 1889, p. 510) Tenney Frank (classical historian): "The race of the human animal survives by means of instincts that shaped themselves for that purpose long before rational control came into play. Before out day it has only been at Greece and Rome that these impulses have had to face the obstacle of sophistication." (Frank 1916, p. 704) Benjamin Franklin: "The greater the common fashionable Expence of any Rank of People, the more cautious they are of Marriage. Therefore, Luxury should never be suffer'd to become common." (Franklin 1775, p. 473) Solzhenitsyn: "Even biology tells us that a high degree of habitual well-being is not advantageous to a living organism. Today, well-being in the life of Western society has begun to take off its pernicious mask." (Berman 1980, p. 7)

How do we account for this allegedly maladaptive response to luxury by the human organism? The sociobiologist asks how it might have been adaptive in the conditions under which it originally evolved. Lorenz, for example, presents the following evolutionary model of this response: "At the time of its probable origin humanity eked out a precarious existence. Hence it bears all the marks of a selection pressure working in the direction of the utmost economy. At the dawn of humanity, men could not afford to pay too high a price for anything. They *had* to be extremely reluctant to make any expenditure of any kind of energy, of risk, or of possessions. Any possible gain had to be greedily seized upon. Laziness, gluttony, and some other present-day vices were virtues then. To shun everything disagreeable, like cold, danger, muscular exertion and so on, was the wisest thing they could do. Life was hard enough to exclude all danger of becoming too 'soft.' These were the circumstances to which our mechanism balancing pleasure and displeasure has been adapted in evolution. They must be kept in mind in order to understand its present miscarriage." (Lorenz 1970, pp. 978-979) Barkow and Burley's model is similar in spirit to that of Lorenz.

entirely fortuitous reasons), since it causes a reduction in the self-destructively high overall population growth rate also attendant upon modernization, but they fail to note the potentially dysgenic effect on the species of this behavior.(9) As noted above, their model predicts that the greater the intelligence of the woman, the more capable she is of avoiding conception and the more able she is to locate niches in the society which provide her with the autonomy required to withstand pressures from kin and males to reproduce. In short, Burley and Barkow's model predicts precisely the inverse relationship between fertility and I.Q. observed today in the U.S. as well as the fertility differentials by economic and social class in both the U.S. and Europe observed since the demographic transition began, with the brief exception of a 10 to 20 year period after World War II. This latter burst of fertility, which was particularly marked among the upper classes, remains, as far as I know, unexplained (Easterlin 1980, p. 277).

The absence in Japan of this inverse relationship suggests that female autonomy is not yet prevalent there, which certainly is in accord with the available statistical data for Japan as well as casual observation of the relations between the sexes there. Female earnings as a percentage of male earnings are lower in Japan (55%) than in the U.S. (61%) and much lower than in West Europe (between 70% and 90%) (*Japan Statistical Yearbook 1981*, p. 416; *Statistical Abstract of the United States 1981*, p. 407; Manley & Sawbridge 1980, p. 37). "Despite

(9) A few students of population in the West, such as Hardin (1972), Bajema (1978), and Weyl (1973), as well as several Chinese demographers (see, for a bibliography, Tien 1981), have flagged this possible "contradiction" in ZPG, but in general it has received scant attention from mainstream demographers and population scientists, as has the subject of population quality more generally. This is despite the fact that the goal of the Population Associatión of America (PAA) is defined in its constitution as the study of population in its "quantitative and qualitative aspects," and that for a number of years the PAA's *Population Index* classified articles under the heading of "policy on quality." The classification, however, is moribund and no longer appears in the *Population Index*'s Table of Contents. In short, the subject of population quality has disappeared from the map of American demography (but not entirely from that of economics, see Kuznets (1974) for a modern revival of Fisher's model, though in somewhat disguised form). The only trace left of it is as a kind of relic word in the PAA's charter. In my view, this silence is not because American demographers deem the subject unimportant but rather because of its association in so many persons' minds with eugenics (indeed, many of the PAA's founders *were* eugenicists, Kiser 1981) and the interest shown in the latter by National Socialists and the members of other extreme right wing movements (Vukowich 1971, *Harvard Law Review* 1981), the implied association with which in turn could potentially harm one's career and standing in scholarly circles.

relatively high educational attainment," writes Linda Martin, "women in Japan still face considerable discrimination in employment and promotion opportunities, wage determination, and retirement practices. When they enter the labor force after completing their education, most women are considered only temporary workers; lifetime employment is not expected or encouraged." (Martin 1982, p. 37) That is, the Barkow-Burley model explains the absence of a dysgenic distribution of births in Japan by the absence of female autonomy in that country. At the same time, it predicts that if the status of women were to improve there, then its first impact might be on the pattern of fertility differentials. There are signs that the rate of participation by women in the labor force has begun to rise in Japan, after a long period of decline unique in the developed world (Martin 1982), and, perhaps not coincidentally, the fertility rate to fall, also after a long period of stability unusual in the developed world (Figure 2).(10) If the Barkow-Burley model is correct, then these shifts should be accompanied by a pattern of fertility differentials closer to that of the West, since they suggest an increase in autonomy among Japanese women, of which the more intelligent and the better endowed economically among them will, on average, take the most advantage. That is, a dysgenic pattern of births should emerge in Japan as it has elsewhere when and if females there achieve a measure of autonomy, though it is not clear that this pattern would be as severe as in the West, given the possibly greater genetic homogeneity of the Japanese and therefore the possibly smaller genetic variability in Japan for natural selection to work with (Freedman 1979).

Conclusion and Summary

Fisher's model of civilization decline has been found wanting in several respects: it assumes a high heritability in fertility and

(10) Nohara-Atoh (1981b), in a comment on Kikuchi (1980), attributes the rapid decrease in the net reproduction rate of Japanese women since about 1973 to the rapid increase in the number of young women postponing child-bearing to later years in order to attend college and argues that the fertility rate will eventually rise back up to replacement levels as these women move into the later years of child-bearing; but there has been as yet no notable increase in the birth rate of older women predicted by this hypothesis. Kikuchi's hypothesis is, by contrast, that Japan is now experiencing, at something of a lag to that of the U.S. and Europe (see Figure 2), a new, permanent level of below replacement fertility. So far, there is no evidence to refute Kikuchi's interpretation of the data, or to support that of Nohara-Atoh.

a low fertility among the upwardly mobile, neither of which appears to be borne out by the data. That the fertility of the upper classes has managed to equal that of the nation as a whole during at least one period of modern history likewise demonstrates that it is not lower biological fecundity, contrary to Fisher's model, which is at the origin of the upper classes' generally lower fertility. However, despite Fisher's misrepresentation of the origins of the differential birth rate across classes, this differential does appear to be a persistent feature of modern, industrial nations, and this differential could have consequences for the distribution of genotypes in a population.

I have made particular application here of the genetic model to explain at least part of the recently recognized gap between the arithmetic means of the I.Q. distributions of Japan and the U.S. as well as Great Britain (Lynn 1977, 1982; Lynn & Dziobon 1980). Fisher's model suggests one partial source of this gap: a difference in the pattern of fertility differentials across classes in Japan and the West, a difference we do observe now. If we can further assume that during periods of high constant fertility, birth differentials by class are negligible, then this difference may well have existed for up to 180 years, since the decline in Japanese fertility occurred comparatively recently with great abruptness, whereas in the West it was gradual and smooth, broken only by a couple of 10-20 year reversals of trend; over the 19th and 20th centuries. 180 years, or six generations, is sufficient to produce a not insignificant proportion of the difference in mean I.Q. observed, since the best evidence says that the demographic transition in the West caused a one point drop in mean I.Q. per generation. Note also that the intellectual gap between Japanese and Westerners should continue to grow as long as the characteristic birth differential by class does not emerge in Japan.

The model of fertility suppression presented by Barkow and Burley predicts that a birth differential will emerge in Japan only if female autonomy becomes prevalent there. They argue that women only replace themselves when forced to by pressure from outside and, given freedom not to do so, will typically under-reproduce (see also Badinter 1981).(11) According to

(11) Unwin (1934) describes a similarly relentless and ultimately successful revolt by women in the advanced civilizations against the institution of absolute monogamy, around which, according to Unwin, all civilizations have been built. Absolute monogamy, again according to Unwin, is the only familial institution so far observed

their model, the more intelligent the woman, the more able she will be to find autonomous positions as well as to employ contraceptive devices, in a society where such positions and devices are widely available. The combination of the two gives her the means to thwart outside pressures from kin and males to reproduce as well as to satisfy her own sexual needs. Japanese society has so far only allowed the second, i.e., contraception, to become prevalent and has thereby effected the demographic transition to low aggregate population growth without the usually attendant dysgenic distribution of births across women. There is only the faintest of indications that autonomy is becoming more prevalent among Japanese women. Moreover, the low variance in the quantitative expression of polygenic traits in Japan predicted by Freedman (1979) on the basis of the anthropological record in Japan, would blunt the dysgenic effect that any increase in female autonomy there would otherwise have.

Fisher's model, in combination with that of Barkow and Burley, provides, then, at least a consistent partial explanation for one of the more interesting racial variations to have been recently discovered, i.e., the intelligence gap between Japanese and Westerners. It is less clear, however, that this model can account for the phenomenon for which it was originally designed: national decay and the decline of civilizations. The most telling and so far unanswered criticism of the genetic model of societal change is that it can only account for the long-term direction of societal change, but not its rate, which is usually rapid. Even those biologists who have been most concerned about the potential for genetic deterioration in modern societies have recognized that cultural decay is almost

capable of reducing sexual opportunity to the point where sufficient energy is released to build a civilization. Thus, in both Unwin's and the sociobiological model described here, civilization is inherently unstable, in that it inevitably erodes its own foundations. Unwin unfortunately does not explain why absolute monogamy should be the only familial institution capable of diverting sexual energy into the creation and maintenance of a civilization. That populations have not discovered more stable methods than absolute monogamy of releasing such energy for expansive and creative purposes, given the obviously great selective advantages of doing so, is a puzzle. Unwin himself did not seem aware of this Darwinian paradox at the heart of his model. As I mentioned above, the sociobiological model likewise does not explain why modernization engenders female autonomy, at least in the West. Such cultural facts are beyond this model's purview. Both models, therefore, as models of civilization decline, are theoretically incomplete.

always much more rapid than genetic decay. Konrad Lorenz, in a recent paper, for example, presents the following apostasy:

> "By the very achievements of his mind, man has eliminated all those selecting factors which have *made* that mind. It is only to be expected that humaneness will presently begin to decay, culturally and genetically, and it is not surprising at all that the symptons of this decay become progressively more apparent on all sides. I may have changed my mind quite a bit concerning the relative importance of cultural and genetical dehumanization; the former proceeds faster by so much that one might regard the second as a rather unimportant *cura posterior.* This change of priority in my opinion was admittedly caused by Roszak [the author of *Making of a Counter Culture*], who has thoroughly frightened me with his convincing exposition of the dehumanizing effects of technocracy. However, the genetic "domestication" of civilized man is, I am convinced, progressing quite rapidly."(12) (Lorenz 1976, p. 126)

Hermann Muller, the eminent geneticist and eugenicist, towards the end of his life likewise recognized the "creeping pace" of dysgenic trends as compared to the "fast growing menaces presented by our cultural imbalances" (Muller 1973, p. 128).

Such cultural imbalances, of course, could be simply the hypertrophic expression of much smaller genetic changes, as Raymond Cattell suggests. We should not underestimate the effect of small changes in the mean value of a trait in a population, according to Cattell, because of "(1) the possible phenomena of emergents ..., i.e., the interactions in a group all of I.Q. 105 may produce considerable differences in group behaviour from interactions in a group of I.Q. 100 ... (2) If most creative leadership comes from those above an I.Q. of, say, 130, the absolute number in this group (with a normal distribution) changes to a greater degree with relatively small changes in the mean." (Cattell & Brennan 1981, pp. 336-337) However, as noted above, there is evidence for the recent past that genetic and cultural changes have actually been in *opposite* directions. Hypertrophy and nonlinear amplification cannot as yet translate a negative change into a positive one, or vice-versa. And

(12) Unfortunately, Lorenz does not tell us what it is he is convinced by, and this failure by Lorenz to be concrete on so momentous an hypothesis is the object of Campbell's most telling criticism (Campbell 1976).

even the small differences used by Cattell in his example take several generations to appear, whereas significant cultural change can take place within the space of a single generation. The postulation of non-linear amplification of genetic change, therefore, does not appear to be a sufficient explanation of either the short-term direction or the pace of change in modern human societies.

The special characteristics of the Japanese people and nation may be especially resistant to the erosive forces, both cultural and genetic, which industrialism has set in motion in the West (Gordon 1982). The strength of this immunity, if it is such, its sources, both genetic and cultural, and their relative importance, should be subjects of abiding interest to students of mankind. The rapid development and industrial dominance of Japan confer upon these subjects a certain importance as well.

REFERENCES

Anonymous
1981 The changing pattern of differential fertility. *The Eugenics Society Bulletin*, 13, 113-114.

Arrow, K.
1975 Thorstein Veblen as economic theorist. *American Economist*, 19, 5-9.

Atsuhiro, S.
1980 Inscrutable epigenetics of the Japanese brain: a book review. *Journal of Social and Biological Structures*, 3, 255-266.

Aymans, G.
1980 The unanimous society – remarks on the generative behaviour of the Japanese society in an extraordinary year. *Geo Journal*, 4, 215-230.

Badinter, E.
1981 The Myth of Motherhood. London: Souvenir Press.

Bajema, C.
1963 Estimation of the direction and intensity of natural selection in relation to human intelligence by means of the intrinsic rate of natural increase. *Eugenics Quarterly*, 10, 175-187.
1978 Genetic implications of population control. In W. Reich, Ed., Encyclopedia of Bioethics, Vol. 3. New York: Free Press, pp. 1307-1311.

Barkow, J. and N. Burley
1980 Human fertility, evolutionary biology, and the demographic transition. *Ethology and Sociobiology*, 1, 163-180.

Befu, H.
1971 *Japan: An Anthropological Introduction.* San Francisco: Chandler.

Berger, B.
1978 A new interpretation of the I.Q. controversy. *Public Interest,* 50, 29-44.

Berman, R.
1980 Solzhenitysn at Harvard, The Address, Twelve Early Responses, and Six Later Reflections. Washington, D.C.: Ethics and Public Policy Center.

Bouchard, T. and M. McGue
1981 Familial studies of intelligence: a review. *Science,* 212, 1055-1059.

Boyd, R. and P. Richerson
1981 Culture, biology and the evolution of variation between human groups. In M. Collins, I. Wainer, and T. Bremmer, Eds., Science and the Question of Human Inequality, AAAS Selected Symposium 58. Boulder: Westview Press, pp. 99-152.

Broadhurst, P., D. Fulker and J. Wilcock
1974 Behavioral genetics. *Annual Review of Psychology,* 25, 389-415.

Burley, N.
1979 The evolution of concealed ovulation. *The American Naturalist,* 114, 835-858.

Campbell, D.
1976 Reintroducing Konrad Lorenz to psychology. In R. Evans, Konrad Lorenz – The Man and His Ideas. New York: Harcourt Brace Jovanovich, pp. 88-118.

Cattell, R.
1972 A New Morality from Science: Beyondism. New York: Pergamon.
1974 Differential fertility and normal selection for I.Q.: some required conditions in their investigation. *Social Biology,* 20, 168-177.

Cattell, R. and J. Brennan
1981 Population intelligence and national syntality dimensions. *Mankind Quarterly,* 21, 327-340.

Cliquet, R. and J. Balcaen
1979 Intelligentie, gezinsplanning en gezinsvorming. *Bevolking en Gezin,* 3, 311-353.

Cliquet, R. and G. Delmotte
1981 Possible effects of alternatives in family size variation in talent-assorting societies. Paper presented to International Union of Societies for the Study of Population 1981 General Conference, Manila, December 9-16.

Coon, C.
1965 The Living Races of Man. New York: Alfred Knopf.

Corning, P.
1972 Discussion: continuing evolution of man, session IV. *Social Biology*, 19, 259-265.

Cummings, W.
1977 The effects of Japanese schools. In A. Kloskowska and G. Martinotti, Eds, Education in a Changing Society. London: Sage, pp. 255-290.
1980 Education and Equality in Japan. Princeton: Princeton University Press.

De Fries, J.
1968 Quantitative genetics and behavior: overview and perspective. In J. Hirsch, Ed., Behavior-Genetic Analysis. New York: Mc Graw-Hill, pp. 322-339.

De Vos, G. and C. Lee
1981 Koreans and Japanese. In C. Lee and G. De Vos, Eds., Koreans in Japan. Berkeley: University of California Press, pp. 3-30.

De Vos, G. and H. Wagatsuma
1966 Japan's Invisible Race. Berkeley: University of California Press.

Dobzhansky, T.
1973 Genetic Diversity and Human Equality. New York: Basic Books.

Duncan, O.
1952 Is the intelligence of the general population declining? *American Sociological Review*, 17, 401-407.

Easterlin, R.
1980 American population since 1940. In M. Feldstein, Ed., The American Economy in Transition. Chicago: University of Chicago Press, pp. 275-321.

Eckland, B.
1967 Genetics and sociology: a reconsideration. *American Sociological Review*, 32, 173-193.

Ehrlich, P. and S. Feldman
1977 The Race Bomb. New York: Quadrangle/The New York Times Book Co.

Eugenics Review
1931 Eugenics in Japan. *Eugenics Review*, 22, 273.

Eysenck, H.
1973 The Measurement of Intelligence. Baltimore: Williams and Wilkins.

Falconer, D.
1966 Genetic consequences of selection pressure. In J. Meade and A. Parkes, Eds., Genetic and Environmental Factors in Human Ability. Edinburgh: Oliver & Boyd, pp. 219-232.

Fisher, R.
1926 Eugenics: can it solve the problem of the decay of civilization? *Eugenics Review*, 18, 128-136.
1958 The Genetical Theory of Natural Selection, 2nd Edition. New York: Dover.

Frank, T.
1916 Race mixture in the Roman empire. *American Historical Review,* 21, 689-708.

Franklin, B.
1755 Observations concerning the increase of mankind, peopling of countries, etc. *Gentlemen's Quarterly,* November; Reprinted in *Perspectives in Biology and Medicine,* 13 (Summer 1970), pp. 469-475.

Freedman, D.
1979 Human Sociobiology. New York: The Free Press.

Garmon, L.
1982 Japanese jump. *Science News,* 122, 28-29.

Godfrey, L. and K. Jacobs
1981 Gradual, autocatalytic and punctuational models of hominid brain evolution: a cautionary tale. *Journal of Human Evolution,* 10, 255-272.

Gordon, R.
1982 Why U.S. wage and employment behaviour differs from that in Britain and Japan. *Economic Journal,* 92, 13-44.

Gottesman, I.
1968 Biogenetics of race and class. In M. Deutsch, I. Katz, and A. Jensen, Eds., Social Class, Race, and Psychological Development. New York: Holt, Rinehart, and Winston, pp, 11-51.

Haldane, J.
1956 Alfred Kinsey. *Hindu Weekly Review,* October 8. Reprinted in C. Christenson, Kinsey – A Biography. Bloomington, Indiana: Indiana University Press, pp. 228-230.

Hardin, G.
1972 Genetic consequences of cultural decisions in the realm of population. *Social Biology,* 19, 350-361.

Harvard Law Review
1981 Eugenic artificial insemination: a cure for mediocrity? *Harvard Law Review,* 94, 1850-1870.

Higgins, J., E. Reed and S. Reed
1962 Intelligence and family size: a paradox resolved. *Eugenics Quarterly,* 9, 84-90.

Huntington, E.
1912 Geographical environment and Japanese character. *Journal of Race Development,* 2, 256-281.

Huxley, J.
1963 Eugenics in evolutionary perpective. *Perspectives in Biology and Medicine,* 6, 155-187.

Jencks, C.
1972 Inequality. New York: Basic Books.

Jensen, A.
1969 How much can we boost IQ and scholastic achievement? *Harvard Educational Review,* 39, 1-123.
1980 Bias in Mental Testing. New York: Basic Books.
1981a Straight Talk about Mental Tests. New York: The Free Press.

1981b Obstacles, problems, and pitfalls in differential psychology. In S. Scarr, Race, Social Class, and Individual Differences in I.Q. Hillsdale, N.J.: Lawrence Erlbaum Associates, pp. 483-514.

Karlsson, J.

1978 The Inheritance of Creative Intelligence. Chicago: Nelson-Hall.

Kikuchi, Y.

1980 A note for sociological population studies – focusing on recent declining fertility in Japan. *Japanese Sociological Review,* 31 (1), 77-84.

Kirk, D.

1957 The fertility of a gifted group: a study of the number of children of men in Who's Who. In The Nature and Transmission of the Genetic and Cultural Characteristics of Human Populations. New York: Milbank Memorial Fund, pp. 78-98.

Kiser, C.

1981 The role of the Milbank Memorial Fund in the early history of the Association. *Population Index,* 47, 490-494.

Koya, Y.

1957 Family planning among Japanese on public relief. *Eugenics Quarterly,* 4, 17-23.

Kuznets, S.

1974 Income-related differences in natural increase: bearing on growth and distribution of income. In P. David and M. Reder, Eds., Nations and Households in Economic Growth: Essays in Honor of Moses Abramovitz. New York: Academic, pp. 127-146.

Lee, C.

1981 The legal status of Koreans in Japan. In C. Lee and G. De Vos, Eds, Koreans in Japan. Berkeley: The University of California Press, pp. 133-158.

Lerner, I.

1968 Heredity, Evolution, and Society. San Francisco: W.H. Freeman.

Lewontin, R.

1970 Further remarks on race and the genetics of intelligence. *Bulletin of Atomic Scientists,* 26, 23-25.

Lohr, S.

1982 Japan struggling with itself – the traits behind the 'miracle' impose their limits. *The New York Times,* June 13, Section 3, pp. 1 and 6.

Lorenz, K.

1970 The enmity between generations and its probable ethological causes. *Studium Generale,* 23, 963-997.

1976 Konrad Lorenz responds to Donald Campbell. In R. Evans, Konrad Lorenz – The Man and His Ideas. New York: Harcourt Brace Jovanovich, pp. 119-128.

Lumsden, C. and E. Wilson

1981 Genes, Mind, and Culture: The Coevolutionary Process. Cambridge, Mass.: Harvard University Press.

Lynn, R.
1977 The intelligence of the Japanese. *Bulletin of British Psychological Society*, 30, 69-72.
1982 I.Q. in Japan and the United States shows a growing disparity. *Nature*, 297, 222-223.

Lynn, R. and J. Dyziobon
1980 On the intelligence of the Japanese and other Mongoloid peoples. *Personality and Individual Differences*, 1, 95-96.

McClearn, G.
1970 Behavioral genetics. *Annual Review of Genetics*, 4, 437-468.

Manley, P. and D. Sawbridge
1980 Women at work. *Lloyds Bank Review*, 135, 29-40.

Martin, L.
1982 Japanese response to an aging labor force. *Population Research and Policy Review*, 1, 19-42.

Matsunaga, E.
1968 Birth control policy in Japan: a review from the eugenic standpoint. *Japanese Journal of Human Genetics*, 13, 189-200.

Mosk, C.
1979 The decline of marital fertility in Japan. *Population Studies*, 33, 19-38.

Muller, H.
1973 What genetic course will man steer? In E. Carlson, Ed., Man's Future Birthright – Essays on Science and Humanity by H.J. Muller. Albany: State University of New York Press, pp. 117-152.

Nisot, T.
1929 La Question Eugénique dans les Divers Pays, Vol. 2. Brussels: Georges Van Campenhout.

Nohara-Atoh, M.
1980 Social Determinants of Reproductive Behavior in Japan. Ph.D. Dissertation, University of Michigan, Ann Arbor, Michigan.
1981a Social determinants of marital fertility in Japan. *Journal of Population Problems*, 157, 1-27.
1981b On the recent fertility decline in Japan. *Japanese Sociological Review*, 31 (4), 91-97.

O'Connell, M.
1981 Regional fertility patterns in the United States: convergence or divergence. *International Regional Science Review*, 6, 1-14.

Olneck, M. and B. Wolfe
1980 Intelligence and family size: another look. *Review of Economics and Statistics*, 62, 241-247.

Osborn, F.
1940 Preface to Eugenics. New York: Harper.

Osborn, F. and C. Bajema
1972 The eugenic hypothesis. *Social Biology*, 19, 337-345.

Osborne, R.
1975 Fertility, I.Q. and school achievement. *Psychological Reports*, 37, 1067-1073.

Pinnelli, A.
1967 La fecondità differenziale: rassegna delle indagini (parte prima). *Genus,* 23, 247-305.

Roberts, J.
1971 Intellectual development of children as measured by the WISC. Washington, D.C.: Department of Health, Education, and Welfare.

Shuckburg, E.
1889 The Histories of Polybius, Vol. 2. Translated from the text of F. Hultsch. London: MacMillan.

Sly, D. and S. Richards
1972 The fertility of a sample of American elites. *Social Biology,* 19, 393-400.

Smith, R.
1981 Fertility, economy, and household formation over three centuries. *Population and Development Review,* 7, 595-622.

Steiner, J.
1938 Japanese population policies. *American Journal of Sociology,* 43, 717-733.

Stevens, G.
1981 Social mobility and fertility. *American Sociological Review,* 46, 573-584.

Tabah, L.
1976 Rapport sur les relations entre la fecondité et la condition sociale et économique de la famille en Europe: leurs répercussions sur la politique sociale. In Council of Europe, European Population Conference, Strasbourg, 31 August - 1 September 1971, Official Documents of the Conference, Vol. I, 1971. Nendeln/Liechtenstein: Kraus Reprint.

Thorndike, R.
1977 Causation of Binet I.Q. decrements. *Journal of Educational Measurement,* 14, 197-202.

Tien, H.
1981 Demography in China: from zero to now. *Population Index,* 47, 683-710.

Tsubouchi, Y.
1970 Changes in fertility in Japan by region: 1920-1965 *Demography,* 7, 121-134.

Udry, J.
1978 Differential fertility by intelligence: the role of birth planning. *Social Biology,* 25, 10-14.

United Nations
1976 Demographic Yearbook 1975. New York: United Nations.

U.S. Bureau of the Census
1980 Fertility of American Women: June 1979. Current Population Reports, Series P-20, No. 358. Washington, D.C.: U.S. Government Printing Office.

Unwin, J.
1934 Sex and Culture. Oxford: Oxford University Press.

Veblen, T.
1915a The opportunity of Japan. *Journal of Race Development*, 6, 23-38.
1915b Imperial Germany and the Industrial Revolution. New York: MacMillan.

Vining, D.
1982 On the possibility of the reemergence of a dysgenic trend with respect to intelligence in American fertility differentials. *Intelligence*, 6, 241-264.

Vukowich, W.
1971 The dawning of the brave new world – legal, ethical, and social issues of eugenics. University of Illinois Legal Forum, No. 2, 189-231.

Waller, J.
1971 Differential reproduction: its relation to IQ test score, education, and occupation. *Social Biology*, 18, 122-136.

Weinrich, J.
1978 Are humans maximizing reproductive success? The author replies. *Behavioral Ecology and Sociobiology*, 3, 97-98.

Westoff, C.
1974 The populations of the developed countries. *Scientific American*, 231 (September), 108-121.

Weyl, N.
1973 Population control and the anti-eugenic ideology. *Mankind Quarterly*, 14, 63-82.
1978 World population growth and the geography of intelligence. *Modern Age*, 22, 64-71.

Whelpton, P.
1949 From eugenic abortion and sterlization to control of conception in Japan. *Eugenical News*, 34, 44-45.

Williams, L. and B. Williams
1974 A re-examination of the heritability of fertility in the British peerage. *Social Biology*, 21, 225-231.

Wilson, E.
1978 On Human Nature. Cambridge, Mass.: Harvard University Press.

Wrong, D.
1980 Class Fertility Trends in Western Nations. New York: Arno.

Yanaga, C.
1949 Japan since Perry. New York: McGraw-Hill.

Yasuda, S.
1969 Samurai descendants and social mobility. *Japanese Sociological Review*, 19 (4), 21-40.

Zajonc, R.
1976 Family configuration and intelligence. *Science*, 192, 227-236.

Zajonc, R. and J. Bargh
1980 Birth order, family size, and decline of SAT scores. *American Psychologist*, 35, 662-668.

POPULATION INTELLIGENCE AND NATIONAL SYNTALITY DIMENSIONS

RAYMOND B. CATTELL and JERRY M. BRENNAN
University of Hawaii

The authors further develop the concept of national 'personality' or syntality, incorporating the concept of population intelligence, and consider methods for making valid cross cultural comparisons of syntality.

The Model of Population-Syntality Relations

The term *syntality* was introduced as the equivalent in an organized group of *personality* in the individual (Cattell, 1966). Assuming that a wide span of behaviors in either are factored we finish with functionally unitary traits a profile of scores on which describe uniquely a given personality or a given syntality. If the groups entering the calculation are nations we are then describing in universal terms the culture pattern of that nation. (Later one can group nations into larger historical "civilizations," in Toynbee's (1947) sense, by the pattern similarity coefficients among national syntality profiles, as recently done by Cattell & Brennan (1981)).

The difference between a syntality and a population characteristic is that the former is scored on some organized behavior of the group as a whole, e.g. the number of treaties it makes, the GNP, the frequency of its involvement in war, its plan for welfare, etc., while the latter is a mean of the population e.g. in age, in number of children per family, in intelligence score. The line has not been easy to draw between these and the scores on syntality factors have often been found to contain population measures e.g. frequency of divorce, per annum expenditure on education (Cattell, Breul & Hartman, 1952; Cattell, Graham & Woliver, 1979).

The theoretical model supposes that any syntal act or performance is a function, just as in the personality behavioral equation, of scores on syntality factors, S_1 to S_k, and factor analytically obtained "behavioral weights," b's, peculiar to the factor S_x and to the performance j. Thus

$$a_{ij} = b_{j1}S_{1i} + b_{j2}S_{2i} + \ldots + b_{jk}S_{ki} \qquad [1]$$

where i is the individual nation or other group concerned. These b's are functions of the nature of the act and the situation in which it is performed. For example, the act of involvement in war proved (in the 1936-1936 period) to be weighted largely on two or three syntality factors thus:

Frequency of Involvement = .6A + .3B -.4C.
where A is the factor called "cultural pressure with intolerance of burden" (Cattell, Graham & Woliver, 1979); B is "affluence"; and C is an uninterpreted factor loading high artistic and educational support.(From Cattell, 1949).

[2]

The score of a group on a syntality dimension is hypothesized to be a function of the population characters and the group structure, represented by t's. As an initial approximation on which to develop further the model is assumed linear and additive, as in [1] thus

$$S_{xi} = t_{x1}P_{1i} + t_{x2}P_{2i} + \ldots + t_{xn}P_{ni} \qquad [3]$$

where the P's are scores on a population traits for the given group.

Despite the complication of having to enter a systems theory, however, we must assume here a two-way causal action, in that the population characters in part determine the syntality and the syntality in part determines the personality of the population (See, On the theory of group learning, Cattell 1953).For example the intelligence of the population might in part determine the decision to adopt a syntal structure of higher education and the existence of higher education might help determine the average real standard of living in the population. Thus the systems action reciprocal to (3) is:

$$P_{yi} = e_{y1}S_{1i} + e_{y2}S_{2i} + \ldots + e_{yk}S_{ki} \qquad [4]$$

where e's are used to indicate the "educative" action, in the broadest sense of educative, of the cultural syntality traits upon the individual and therefore on the population average.

Only in manipulative experiment (and therefore with small groups in experimental group dynamics) has it been possible as in the work of Asch (1952), Cattell & Stice (1960), Fiedler (1954), Borgatta & Bales (1955) and several others to find the extent of a one way causal action, namely, from personality to syntality, as in [3] By testing on the 16 Personality Factor questionnaire 1000 young men, and *then* measuring the performances of the *neonate* groups in which they were put together, Cattell & Stice (1960) were able to show that there are substantial causal effects of population characters upon group performance. For example, neurotic traits in the population significantly reduced one of the two main morale dimensions of groups. Prior to this Psychologists, with clinical restriction, had theorized more about what the culture does to the neurotic than what the neurotic does to the culture! A generation later this one way thinking is repeating itself in regard to the criminal.

Preliminary Evidence on the Likelihood of Significant Population-Syntality Trait Relationships

With the recent belated but rapid rise in socio-biological science (Wilson, 1979; Lumsden & Wilson, 1981; Cattell, 1972; 1974; Lynn, 1977, 1979; Eysenck, 1971; Darlington, 1969; Pearson, 1981; Hardin, 1977) we get increasingly reminded that some of the P's in equation [3] are likely to be substantially genetic. In this case the largely genetic population traits may affect the cultural syntality, but the cultural syntality will not *immediately* affect that subsection of P's – population traits – in equation [3]. The word "immediately" is necessary because any culture almost certainly in the long run exercises genetic natural selection, very occasionally by deliberate eugenic action, more generally by unrecognized consequences of syntality and structure – as often dysgenic as eugenic. (The reduction of child bearing in more intelligent women through their high employment outside the home relative to the less employable would be a current instance).

The present article throws light on the uncommon case of a population-syntality connection in which there is good reason to believe in a substantial heredity in the population trait – namely, intelligence.

To keep a due sense of the speculative level of present theory in this area let us recognize herewith the sparsity and extreme recency of empirical evidence on personality-syntality connections, regardless of heritability. True, there have been, since Benedict and Mead, considerable expenditures on cross cultural research, but it has been on quite specific cultural customs, and the relations to broader cultural developments have been argued by psychoanalytic and other intuitive approaches. In nine-tenths of this work an insufficient number of cultures and a psychometrically poorly defined and measurable set of variables (often different for each investigator) have been used to permit statistically dependable correlational analysis.

Until 1980 the only factorially defined personality traits entering into such research appear to have been anxiety and intelligence. Cattell & Scheier (1961, p. 274) obtained scores on the same anxiety scale for 6 countries. This being too few for a correlation they speculated that two syntality traits could be at work (1) affluence vs. poverty and (2) conflict of values between major national sub-cultures. By 1969, Cattell, Eber & Tatsuoka (1970, p. 254) had raised to 12 (and soon after to 16) the national samples scored for anxiety and other personality factors. In 1971 Lynn interrelated these anxiety scores in a very interesting manner with various population and syntality scores such as suicide rate, alcoholism, sex customs, and climate and emerged, despite the inevitable "patchiness" of data, with some impressive leads regarding theories of population-syntality relations.

Confirmation of significant correlations across cultures, not only of one population trait with another, but of population and syntality, was obtained on a still larger sample (18 countries) recently by Cattell) Woliver and Graham (1980). Despite the complex causal chain that must commonly exist some of these proved readily understandable in terms of the syntality factor being a relatively direct product of the population factor. For instance, syntality factor 6, intolerance of cultural pressure, marked by frequency of riots and clashes with other countries, correlates significantly with lack of guilt proneness (0 factor) and high surgency (F), i.e. uninhibited temperament, in population measures.

The Syntality Dimensions Hypothesized to Correlate with Population Intelligence

This general setting has called for discussion before approaching the present results which are on the only other unitary trait – intelligence – on which a comparable amount of empirical data has begun to accumulate.

A long backlog of speculative theories awaits testing when such data becomes available. Four syntality factors have been checked as to pattern and speculated upon as related to population intelligence, since their discovery 25 years ago (Cattell, 1949; Cattell, Breul & Hartman, 1952; Cattell, Graham & Woliver, 1979). They are labelled:

1. *Vigorous adapted development-vs-underdevelopment*, load-

ing high industrialization, restriction of birth rate, many calories of food per day per capita, may telephones per capita.

2. *Intelligent affluence* loading variables of education and affluence such as high GNP, much domestic mail per capita, much air travel per capita, high expenditure on education, more Nobel prizes in science, freedom of the press from censorship, etc.

3. *Morality-morale-vs-anarchic anomie.* In the Cattell, Breul & Hartman (1949), Cattell (1949), and Cattell & Gorsuch (1965) studies this stood out as a pure "high morality" factor, loading low murder rates, low drunkenness convictions, low venereal disease, and low typhoid incidence (Community conscience on water supply, etc.). But, either through the lapse of forty years or because the new factoring spans a wider world of cultures, it altered more to an unsophisticated community life with low death rate, low hypertension, etc., as opposed to a sophisticated "anomie."

Cultural Pressure with Sublimation

(The dimension numbers to this point have been the same as in the main replicated list (Cattell, Graham & Woliver, 1979) but we now shift to dimension 8 in that series.) Loads measure of high urbanization, more patents sealed per 100,000, more Nobel prizes in science, high GNP, high ratio of divorces to marriages, much membership of international organizations (governmentally and privately), low ratio early to late marriages, etc.

Factors 1, 2 and 4 overlap appreciably in loaded variables in the area of high energy usage, tertiary to primary occupations, and "highly civilized" characteristics generally. Yet the factor analytic verdict is that there are three distinct factors, and in the earlier discussions those distinct interpretations were started for them which have stood up to subsequent additions. The meaning of the first is that of the level of advance, in different countries, of an historical process of industrialization. The second has evoked theories: (1) That greater expenditure on education is a by-product of affluence through natural resources, (2) That higher education and technology produce greater wealth from an average supply of natural resources, and (3) That, in a world of easy international cultural communication higher levels of education and affluence are alike products of a higher racial population level in intelligence.

The third in this trio, cultural pressure, has received an interesting psychodynamic explanation, recognizing that the complications of high urbanization produce many ergic frustrations. The drives affected, being blocked in both their biological expressions and the outlets for pugnacity arising from the frustration eventually, in part, appear in sublimations in creative arts and sciences. The morality dimension (No.3) needs no special explanation, and is probably tied to earlier religious developments.

It is these four dimensions of syntality that we would, *a priori*, and for reasons discussed more fully below, expect to be related to population intelligence, and in fact it is only these, and a fifth that was unanticipated, that approach significant correlation in the expected direction when correlations of intelligence are worked out (Table 1) with all nineteen syntality dimensions.

In forming the above hypothesis we have also been guided by the preliminary study of Lynn (1979) which seems to be as yet the only one in the field, though Jonassen (1961), and Thorndike (1939) come near to making similar inferences possible. Lynn worked on division of Britain rather than nations, which loses some of the organic causal action of the latter, but gains by leaving no doubt about the comparability of intelligence and educational measures. The cluster of correlations he finds, which includes in positive association population intelligence scores, mean earnings, higher degrees, and memberships of the Royal Society per capita could well be a cluster produced by overlap of the above factors, If anything the causal feedback within districts, not organically separated, might be expected to be less than that which must occur within independent systems, as nations are, to a greater extent. Consequently it has seemed wortwhile to explore for significant relations of population mean intelligence and the four syntality dimensions described in this section.

Results and Discussion

Attempts at cross cultural comparison of intelligence test scores have been very few, and for good reasons. Lynn (1977 b) has made a comparison of American and Japanese populations on the WAIS, finding a mean of 106 for the latter. This is interesting and may be real, but we cannot accept it as reliable evidence because it is hopeless to compare items on a translated traditional crystallized intelligence scale like the WAIS.

Fortunately, culture fair intelligence tests such as the IPAT Scales, the Raven and others have been available for forty years and have gradually had their properties (1) and their degree of culture fairness established. Space precludes the lengthy digressions some critics might wish here so the reader is referred elsewhere (Cattell, 1971, 1979; Horn, 1976) with the observation that (1) culture fairness and freedom from test sophistication are different properties, and the administration must eliminate the latter, (2) differences so far seen have no relation to remoteness of cultures: for example the U.S. Midwest and Taiwan score almost identically on the same form, but north and south Italy (personal communication by Professor L. Meschieri) have appreciable difference, (3) the factor structure of the subtests remains similar in different countries, e.g. the U.S. and Germany (Weiss, 1969).

The identical IPAT four subtest Culture Fair Scale 2 has now been independently standardized in the U.S., Germany, France, Britain, India, Japan and (unpublished) in Taiwan and possibly other countries. A separate report will be prepared on comparisons of these formal standardizations, but they are not numerous enough to give us the correlations needed here. Instead we turn to the recent remarkably extensive sampling with the IPAT Culture Fair Scale 3 by Buj (1981) in 21 European countries. His list (1981, p. 168) we raised to 24 by including the U.S.A., at 100 I.Q. (since the standardization centered thereon), Ghana at 82.2, also from Buj, and Japan at 103 (a compromise of culture fair and Lynn's value). The countries included, for all of which we fortunately have scores on all 19 syntality dimensions were: Austria, Belgium, Bulgaria, Czechoslovakia, Denmark, Finland, France, Germany, Ghana, Great Britain, Greece, Holland, Hungary, Ireland, Italy, Japan, Norway, Poland, Portugal, Spain, Sweden, Switzerland, U.S.A., and Yugoslavia.

Naturally a great deal turns on the sampling procedures and the sample sizes used. They ranged from a low of 75,where the standard error of the mean would be 2.0 to 1572 (Germany) where it would be 0.6 and to the U.S.A. standardization sample 3140) where it would be 0.27. As to procedure Buj balanced for male and female, age and socio-economic states, but naturally in this first collection of such data some "wobble" from ideal sampling has to be accepted. The mean I.Q.'s ranged from 109.4 (Holland) to 82.2 (Ghana). The standard deviations were more variable than would be expected. However, the U.S.A., on which the original standardization was made, stands close (100) to the mean, 101.3, of all 24 countries, which might be expected of a large country based on the melting pot principle.

The correlations with the syntality dimensions described in the last section are given in Table 1.

The correlations with the remaining dimensions are all statistically quite insignificant and, with two exceptions, negligible. They are with F4, -.31; F5, -.18, F6, .06; F7, .02; F9, 0.26; F10, -.07; F11, -.04; F12, .21; F13, .06; F14, .03; F15, .01; F16, .06; F17, -.11; F18, -.06 and F19, -.23, the factor numbers being those given in Cattell, Graham & Woliver (1979). The "suggestions" in the two exceptions are of some positive correlation of intelligence with smallness of country and some negative correlation with Muslim culture. Statistically these are way down at a $P<.15$ and $P<.23$ level (two-tailed).

As Table 1(a) shows, (1) all correlations are in the hypothesized direction of association. Vigorous Adapted Development reaches a commonly accepted standard of significance. Intelligence, Affluence and Morality are not far behind, and can be considered definitely suggestive.

The hypothesis now proposed is that high population intelligence favors all four of these these particular developments, but that historical and environmental circumstances additionally enter into the specific development of each. If that is true there should be a general factor running through them and it should correlate with intelligence more than intelligence does with any single dimension. First we calculated a multiple correlation of the scores on all four dimensions with intelligence, which came out at .40, again significant at the $P<.05$ level. Secondly we looked at the Table 1(b) matrix which, except for a small negative r of variable 3 and 4 is compatible with the existence of a general factor.

The simple structure rotation of the original primary syntality factors, though carried far (Cattell, Graham & Woliver, 1979) was not carried to fixing factor correlations to the level of precision needed for a really accurate second order analysis, so at this point, and with too few variables for fixing a second order simple structure we have not seen fit to factor Table 1(b), but only to take out the first, unrotated, principal component. It proves to load Syntality factor 1, by .78; 2, by .78; 3, by .49; 4, by .64 and intelligence by .58. With the standard errors of r's on 24 cases we cannot conclude that .58 is definitely less then .78, so it remains possible that the common factor to these syntality dimensions *is* the fluid intelligence level. However, with out knowledge of the relation of fluid and crystallized intelligence factors we would hypothesize that these results so far suggest a general fluid intelligence factor through all four plus a crystallized intelligence or other cultural development common mostly to vigorous adapted development and intelligent affluence but present also in cultural pressure.

To develop a well integrated hypothesis here it is necessary to sail into the stormy waters of the debates on inheritance of intelligence and the clash of sociologists and socio-biologists. On the first we believe evidence is now very strong that the population heritability of fluid intelligence, g_f, stands between 60 and 70% and of crystallized intelligence between 40 and 50% (Cattell, 1981). Regarding the second, our opening model accepts that syntality dimensions are determined by both genetic and environmental-historical influences. Additionally the genetic endowments themselves are a product of genetic mutation and environmental selection. Lumsden & Wilson (1981) point to the unprecedented increase of human cranial capacity in the comparatively short period of the ice ages. Severity of natural selection was obviously important but it could not have been effective without a sufficient abundance of mutations. Cattell (1971) has suggested that cultural developments could not infrequently be the consequences of genetic innovations, bringing populations into new environments and, especially, new areas of perception and activity in existing environments. Perhaps the mutual feedback of genetic and environmental actions, as in the ice age illustration, is more common, but the possibility of causal initiative in cultural change must be given to both. This concept, with refined and exciting mathematical model forms, has recently been developed further by Lumsden & Wilson (1981) in what they call "culturgens" which are zones and forms of cultural development dependent upon and conditioned by genetic developments. (The art of painting would make little headway in a population born color blind.) Incidentally we would suggest to these and other socio-biologists that although quite specific cultural

TABLE 1

(a), Correlation of Mean Population 1 (b), with Four Syntality Traits Hypothesized to relate intelligence, and (b), Correlation among Traits.

(a) *Correlations with Population Intelligence*

	r	P (one-tailed)
Vigorous Adapted Development	.34	.05
Intelligent Affluence	.25	.12
Morality-morale	.30	.08
Cultural Pressure with Sublimation	.15	.25

(b) *Correlations Among Syntality Traits and Intelligence*

	1	2	3	4	5
1. Vigorous Adapted Development					
2. Intelligent Affluence	.40				
3. Morality-morale	.27	.37			
4. Cultural Pressure with Sublimation	.48	.47	.15		
5. Population Intelligence	.34	.25	.29	.15	

elements – like painting – may be suitable elements for relating to specific genes, the objectively determined major cultural dimensions in syntality may prove more suitable than specific, narrow, social indicators for relating to the equally objective personality and ability source trait structures in populations.

In the present case of intelligence we should note that (a) If groups are derived from a larger population the breakdown of the variance among group means into genetic and environmental parts would be the same as found for individuals namely 60-70 to 30-40, (b) That in the absence of auxiliary information our best estimate of the genetic intelligence rank is the same as that for the given data, (c) That in all groups – districts, cities, nations, classes, races – yet examined on intelligence tests the within group variance has uniformly proved much greater than the between group mean differences. Nevertheless the latter must not be underestimated because of (1) the possible phenomena of emergents (Cattell, 1938), i.e. the interactions in a group all of I.Q. 105 may produce considerable difference in group behavior from interactions in a group of I.Q. 100. (There probably operates here also the demonstrated *coercion to the bio-social mean* (Cattell, 1981)). (2) If most creative leadership comes from those above an I.Q. of, say, 130, the absolute number in this group (with a normal distribution) changes to a greater degree with relatively small changes in the mean.

Let us note, however, that no matter what one may conceive *a priori* about the importance of mean differences, the correlations obtained here are actually between national syntality scores and means on population intelligence scores. And let us note also that if any noteworthy sources of bias have affected the magnitudes of these correlations the two that are most obvious will have reduced them below true values.

They are (1) the usual attenuation from invalidity in factor estimation (which we must admit to be appreciable because of the changing weights in syntality estimates) from non-comparability of data defined across countries, and the difficulty of getting comparability in Buj's samples, and (2) the restriction of range in that with two exceptions the 24 nations taken for intelligence measures are all 'Western cultures', whereas the 120 countries factored for syntality dimensions are the world's total. Incidentally, a future improvement would also be to get the syntality factor score estimation patterns from refactoring within the subgroup concerned, since Cattell & Brennan's (1982) taxonomic analysis shows such well defined cultural subgroups that the factors within each are likely to deviate from those found in the total population of countries.

In this broader context of considerations, unfortunately not presently reducible to exact statistical corrections but pointing to true values larger than those above, the hypothesis, if not the conclusion, that we draw is that we have here an example of Lumsden & Wilson's culturgen model. The technical-industrial developments in the Vigorous Adapted Development factor; the maintenance of "civilized" living standards in the intelligent Affluence factor; the avoidance of crime and disorder in the Morality factor, and the reaching of creative heights in the arts and sciences in the Cultural Pressure factor, are all aided by a higher level of intelligence in the population, which, in fluid intelligence is substantially genetic. These four different developments – roughly industrial technology, gentlemanly education, appreciation of moral standards and cultural creativity – are each substantially determined by different environmentally-aided, historically-initiated, ongoing processes and traditions, but the levels reached are determined also, in part, by the average general genetic mental capacity levels of the populations involved. As regards syntality trait No. 1, distinguishing adapted development from underdevelopment, if the connection is with the genetic part of g_f, and if culture fair tests should show significantly lower values for certain of the "developing" countries, the practical politician will have to face the fact that, despite full cultural communication, some countries are likely to remain undeveloped, at least for some centuries, relative to the still mounting developmental levels of the present "developed" countries.

REFERENCES

Asch, S.E.
1952 *Social psychology*. New York: Prentice Hall.

Borgatta, E.F., & Bales, R.F.
1955 Interaction of individuals in reconstituted groups. Pp. 379-395 in Borgatta, E.F. (Ed.) Small groups. New York: Knopf.

Buj, V.
1981 Average I.Q. values in various European countries. *Personality and Individual Differences*, 2, 168-169.

Cattell, R.B.
1938 Some changes in social life in a community with a falling intelligence quotient. *British J. of Psychology*, 28, 430-450.

Cattell, R.B.
1949 The dimensions of culture patterns by the factorization of national character. *J. of Abnormal and Social Psychology*, 44, 443-469.
1953 On the theory of group learning. *J. of Social Psychology*, 37, 27-52.
1966 Cultural and political-economic psychology. Chapter 26, Pp. 769-789 in Cattell, R.B. (Ed.) *Handbook of multivariate experimental psychology*. Chicago: Rand McNally.
1971 *Abilities: their structure, growth and action*. Boston: Houghton Mifflin.
1972 *Beyondism: A new morality from science*. New York: Pergamon Press.
1974 Differential fertility and normal selection for I.Q.: some required conditions in their investigation. *Social Biology*, 21, 168-177.
1979 Are culture fair intelligence tests possible and necessary? *J. of Research and Development in Education*, 12, 3-13.
1981 *The inheritance of personality and ability*. New York: Academic Press.

Cattell, R.B. & Brennan, J.
(In press) 1981 The cultural types of modern nations, by two quantitative classification methods.

Cattell, R.B., Eber, H.J., & Tatsuoka, M.
1970 *Handbook to the 16 Personality Factor Questionnaire.* Champaign, Ill., IPAT.

Cattell, R.B. & Gorsuch, R.L.
1965 The definition and measurement of national morale and morality. *J. of Social Psychology*, 67, 77-96.

Cattell, R.B., Graham, R.K., Woliver, R.E.
1979 The cultural grouping of 100 modern nations determined by applying taxonome to syntality profiles. *J. of Social Psychology*, 108, 241-258.

Cattell, R.B. & Scheier, I.H.
1961 *The meaning and measurement of neuroticism and anxiety.* New York: Ronald.

Cattell, R.B. & Stice, G.F.
1960 *The dimensions of groups and their relations to the behavior of members.* Champaign, Ill.: Instit. Person. & Abil. Testing.

Cattell, R.B., Woliver, R.E. & Graham, R.K.
1980 The relation of syntality dimension of modern national cultures to the personality dimensions of their populations. *International J. of Intercultural Relations*, 4, 15-41.

Cattell, R.B., Breul, H. & Hartman, H.P.
1952 An attempt at more refined definition of the cultural dimensions of syntality in modern nations. *American Sociological Review*, 17, 408-421.

Darlington, C.D.
1969 *The evolution of man and society.* New York: Simon & Schuster.

Eysenck, H.J.
1971 The I.Q. argument. New York: Library Press.

Fiedler, F.E.
1954 Assumed similarity measures as predictors of team effectiveness. *J. Abnormal & Social Psychology*, 49, 381-388.

Graham, R.K.
The future of man. Quincy, Mass.: Christopher Publishing House.

Hardin, G.
1977 *The limits of altruism: an ecologist's view of survival.* Bloomington: Indiana University Press.

Horn, J.L.
1976 Human abilities; a review of research and theories in the early 1970's. *Annual Review of Psychology*, 27, 457-485.

Jonassen, C.F.
1961 Functional unities in 88 community systems. *American Sociological Review*, 26, 399-407.

Lumsden, C.J. & Wilson, E.O.
1981 *Genes, mind and culture: the evolutionary process.* Cambridge, Mass.: Harvard University Press.

Lynn, R.
1977(a) Selective migration and the decline of intelligence in Scotland. *Social Biology*, 24, 173-182.

1977(b) *Psychological Society*, 30, 69-72.
1979 *British J. of Social and Clinical Psychology*.

Pearson, R.
1981 *Ecology and evolution*. Washington, D.C.: Mankind Quarterly Monogr. No. 1.

Thorndike, E.L.
1939 *Human nature and the social order*. New York: Macmillan.

Toynbee, A.A.
1947 *A study of history*. New York: Oxford University Press.

Weiss, R.H.
196 *Die Brauchbarkeit des Culture Free Intelligence Test Skala 3 (CFT3) bei begabungs-psychologischen. Untersuchungen*. Diss. University of Würzberg

Wilson, E.O.
1975 *Sociobiology: the new synthesis*. Cambridge, Mass.:Belknap Press of Harvard University Press.

APPENDIX

SOME CHANGES IN SOCIAL LIFE IN A COMMUNITY WITH A FALLING INTELLIGENCE QUOTIENT

By RAYMOND B. CATTELL

From "The British Journal of Psychology,"
Vol. XXVIII, Part 4, April 1938.

I. Origin of the problem

From a recently completed survey (5, 7) of reproduction rates obtaining at various levels of intelligence in the population of Great Britain, I have drawn the conclusion that, at the present moment, the average level of native mental capacity is falling at the rate of approximately one point of I.Q. per decade.

This conclusion depends upon two premises: (1) that throughout the whole intelligence range the average size of family for each intelligence class is inversely related to the intelligence level, and (2) that, although the gene complex determining individual intelligence is far from being understood, the facts of psychological measurement indicate that, even for quite small groups, intelligence of children may be predicted from intelligence of parents, as if mental capacity were a product of heredity.

Though the observation that mental capacity is largely inborn has long been accepted by the majority of psychologists, it has not always been so favourably received by workers in sister sciences. The truth of the observation need not be discussed afresh here, since the evidence up to date has been comprehensively summarized elsewhere (6), but it is relevant to point out that even the most generous allowance for environment which those wishing to stress environment have dared to claim, would fail to account for more than a small fraction of the variability of intelligence quotient existing in our population.

Calculations of the differential birth-rate based on surveys in rural or urban areas remote in space or culture from those investigated in this first enquiry, or separated by an interval of time sufficient to permit of changes in birth-control practice, may cause us to modify the above figure for rate of decline. Consequently the present study will not depend upon the assumption that the figures are accurate. Indeed it will not depend for its *raison d'être* on the assumption that any decline at all has been proved, but will take its justification from the fact that the relation of community mental capacity to social and cultural habits has been grievously neglected in both discussion and investigation, in spite of its great theoretical and practical interest.

Should the above survey be confirmed in its findings, this hypothetical treatment of the relation of culture to the biological quality of the units constituting the group would become relevant to practical politics, for the methods of combating the decline must depend upon a sound analysis of cause and effect among the conditions accompanying it.

II. Limits of the discussion

Social consequences might conceivably follow either from changes in the absolute level of intelligence, the distribution form remaining constant, or from changes in distribution, e.g. standard deviation, the average level remaining unchanged.

Both kinds of change appear to be taking place, for a bulge in the distribution curve at the 70–90 I.Q. level would increase standard deviation if, as seems likely, the upper intelligence levels are passing out of the phase of greatest family restriction; but in a first attack on the problem it seems best to limit the discussion largely to the downward shift of the distribution curve as a whole.

To argue that certain social changes must of scientific necessity follow the posited changes in biological character is not to expect that they will do so as a matter of historical fact. For intelligence is only one of many independent factors, and the cultural influences among the latter, e.g. the influences of individual leaders, are more rapid and unpredictable in action though, of course, their action is itself modified by the factor we have to consider here. Secondly, the primary social and economic consequences of the intelligence change will interact among themselves, masking, transmuting and producing consequences of a second order. These consequences are too numerous and complex to be discussed in a first study. Moreover it would be premature to attack them until the first set of direct consequences has been approved by argument and research. Except in rare instances the discussion will therefore confine itself to the first and direct influences of a falling intelligence level.

III. Methods of solution

To look for the effects entirely, or even mainly, in the cognitive field—in educational, academic and technical industrial efficiency—merely because the variable we are dealing with is a cognitive one, would produce an altogether false solution of the problem.

Clinical experience has convinced the present writer that the researches of, for example, Burt (1), Healy (10) and Terman (16), showing mental capacity to be one of the more important factors determining the individual's character development, tend to understate, by simplifying, the extent to which character education is limited and modified by the individual's mental capacity. If this is true of the individual, it must apply even more powerfully in society, which to a far greater extent creates its own environment. For, apart from the heritage of skills and intellectual furniture handed down from previous cultures and now almost constant the world over, the mental capacities of the members of a group (and whatever other psychological qualities, if any, are fixed by inheritance) are themselves the environment shaping the formation of character and limiting the patterns of emotional adjustment in living individuals and in the coming generation. It is true that this heritage, which may seem disposed of over-lightly in the above sentence, includes the use made of the (constant) physical world and also the economic system, its level of energy supply and its structure. But these, in a community which has long had various alternatives open to its choice, must in the end be selected largely according to the community intelligence level.

The fields in which these effects will be felt and their particular character must, of course, in the end be decided by experimental and statistical methods, like any other problem of social psychology. Suitable experimental situations may not easily be found, for groups of differing intelligence average generally differ also in racial type and cultural history, whilst to pick out groups within the same race and nation does not provide all the conditions required, for such groups would rarely have had any extensive control over their own legal, economic and social customs. Studies of a sufficient number of groups, even if differing racially and in social heritage, should, however, permit some general conclusions to be drawn, just as the gathering of data on a sufficient number of individuals will enable one to eliminate all individual differences other than that to be studied.

There is no reason why valid answers to some issues should not emerge from experimental study on a relatively small scale of groups of children, equated in age and other respects but differing by a known amount in average I.Q. or standard deviation within the group. Observations could be made on the qualitative differences in their manners of organization, rules, customs and moral standards. Quantitative results could be obtained by comparing their scores in competitive games and community projects; whilst the technique for measuring attitudes, interests and allied questions of energy disposal, would almost certainly yield interesting general laws.

Doubtless the findings would be far more surprising than any to be deduced from armchair analysis. The present writer once had the opportunity of seeing a team of mentally defective youths play at football a team of normals of the same age and weight. The former won rather easily, this result being seemingly due to the fact that, thwarted in mental expression, they had given more time to acquiring physical skills, and also to the more ready renunciation of individual success to which these youths had become accustomed earlier and which gave great solidarity to their team work.

This article, presenting a first approach to the problem, must unfortunately depend largely on deductive reasoning, employing our knowledge of the nature of mental capacity and an analysis of social situations. But there are already, here and there, valuable empirical studies connecting intelligence and behaviour in special fields of social life, and upon these we can draw for the construction of foundations. These fields are the applied sciences of industrial psychology, child guidance, and educational psychology, plus a few specific studies in social psychology. Since the consequences in the educational field are relatively certain and clear cut, and since effects elsewhere to some extent ensue naturally from them, it would be best to consider education first.

IV. Nature of changes deduced

(a) *In education*

Probably the most significant improvement of our educational system during the past decade has been the progress of the precise classification of children according to real ability, extending from the special schools, through the C, B and A classes of the elementary schools, to the A classes of selective secondary schools. In these distinct streams the children proceed at very different rates for, as Burt has shown, the variability in mental age tends to result, at least in some of the main school subjects, in an even greater variability of attainment age.

But of greater significance to society is the fact that in the 'child-centred' school of to-day the curricula and methods are adapted, not only in levels but in quality and range, to the capacities of the children; for interest is a function of capacity and teaching without interest is futile unless tyranny is invoked. This means that any alteration in the numbers of children born at the various intelligence levels will lead inevitably to changes in the proportions of young citizens having the various kinds of training and curricula. To take an instance from one end of the scale: the 24 % increase predicted in the numbers of feeble-minded will result in a similar increase in the school leavers trained only in crude handwork, barely able to read and unable to carry out elementary calculations. The modern child-centred school only serves to bring out more clearly the truth inherent in all educational systems: that the standards and types of education, when the community is giving the best it can to all children, are at the mercy of birth-rates.

This general change, in which those fitted for advanced and abstract studies dwindle whilst those profiting only by simple, concrete education increase, needs next to be considered quantitatively with regard to the maintenance of scholastic standards in all types of school, with their existing curricula and goals. The fall of intelligence with which we have to deal amounts to six months of mental age in a generation. Such a fall might be offset by greater time given to the main subjects of education, either by economising on the unfortunate 'frills' or by increasing the length of school life.

Although the results of education can closely simulate native wit, the product of substitution will not be quite the same.[1] Proficiency in such subjects as arithmetic and English (notably style and vocabulary) correlates much more closely with '*g*' than does proficiency in simple manual and mental skills. Consequently in the former a point is soon reached in the decline of intelligence beyond which insufficient intelligence is compensated for by a quite exorbitant expenditure of time, or not at all. Teachers who complain that an extra year or two of schooling will

[1] As every academic teacher knows, education beyond a student's actual capacity can have a sterilizing effect on the mind and a stultifying effect on personality; but these psychological complications cannot be followed up here. Whilst this article was being written a landlady, describing a visitor to the writer, said, in good faith, "He was an educated man, but not stupid...."

be wasted on a certain proportion of their charges are naturally referring to abstract and conventionally 'cultural' subjects, not to manual skills.

The ultimate consequences in education have not been considered until we look at economic effects. Since the feeble-minded child costs £36 per annum (the residential defective costs far more) against £12 or £13 for the average child, and since at every level the less intelligent pupil costs more (whilst never reaching the same finished level), existing scholastic standards cannot be maintained without deflecting more state expenditure into education. And this sets up a chain of more remote effects through the economic drain upon the other social services.

(*b*) *In economic life*

Recent studies (4, 7) in this country and several in America have provided us with knowledge of the distribution of intelligence in various occupations. There is a definite and significant grading of average I.Q. according to the complexity of the occupations or to the level of rewards to be expected from the occupation.[1] A good deal of overlap in intelligence exists,[2] the lowest quartile of the medical doctors, for example, being at the same level as the highest quartile for precision fitters or shop assistants.

At first sight we might suppose that a fall in the average intelligence quotients, with the distribution form remaining constant, would result in a shortage of men with suitable capacity for the more skilled or 'professional' occupations, and an excess of those able to absorb only that minimum of lore necessary for unskilled labour.

This assumes that in most occupations men have already reached the limits of their educability. Such a saturation point in education has perhaps been reached in the professions, where men fail to be better teachers or doctors not through any lack of training but through their own limitations, but it is scarcely true of, for example, the ranks of unskilled labour, in which, as our scatter diagrams show (4), there is still undoubtedly a fair proportion of men of high capacity not using that capacity.

Because of this last-mentioned fact, the dwindling of the actual supply of natural capacity could easily be met for a generation or more

[1] Substantially the same order is found for the children of fathers in these occupations, but with more overlap between groups, probably owing to the regressive effect of the mothers, a result of incompletely assortative mating.

[2] It would be a mistake to assume that the scatter of 'total effectiveness' is as great as the scatter of '*g*'. Among those successful in teaching, for example, it seems that lower intelligence is systematically associated with better temperamental endowment (2, 4).

by a better utilization of available ability. Gray & Moskinsky (9),[1] among others, have shown that in our school population only about half of those with secondary school ability actually go to secondary schools.

On the other hand a more thorough combing of the school population, a more complete extraction of good ability from the unskilled occupations, may lead to costly inefficiency where we least expect to find it. For it is a mistake to assume that the occupation requiring the longest training is necessarily that requiring the highest general ability. A good foreman or charge hand needs a high level of general intelligence for the complex human and material problems which not infrequently crop up. And even in mechanized factory work, as G. H. Miles (13) has recently pointed out, "countless...operations have arisen which demand little bodily activity and much specialized mental effort and concentration". It may be more important to avoid incompetent surgeons than incompetent railway foremen, and this combing of the population for good brains is indicated also by social justice; but it is not a solution of the problem of declining intelligence, even temporarily.

Though it is obviously untrue to say that in all occupations men are called upon to behave in ways characteristic of their intelligence at its upper limits, they are, in a great number of acts and decisions, working close to this upper limit. Any fall of intelligence might be expected to involve industry in a disproportionate increase in training to compensate for deficiencies or to avoid difficulties which would not have arisen with the more self-sufficient worker.

When such education is not given, or where it is useless to seek in education compensation for the lack of native wit, the result of a heaping up of individuals at a certain low intelligence level will be unemployment at that level. In all branches of industry, commerce and administration, a certain ratio of the number of highly trained to less trained has been established by the nature of the work to be done. The employment of a certain number of men of lesser ability requires the catalysing and directive influence of men more gifted. A falling off in the numbers of the latter means unemployment for the former.

Looking at the matter more broadly, we may say that any given culture establishes a certain distribution curve of demand for intelligence at various levels, and that harmony must exist between this curve and the curve of supply given by the birth-rates at various intelligences.

[1] These workers obtained 42·9% as going to secondary schools, but their age group was from 9·0 to 12·6 years whereas 11 + is the normal age for transferring to a secondary school.

Originally these curves must have been identical, for a society could not invent or borrow a culture more complex than it could understand. But dislocations might take place through alterations in either of the curves. A widespread earthquake, for instance, or a war, by creating immense demands for relatively unskilled labour, would be inappropriate to the present curve of supply (Fig. 1), but any bulge in the lower part of the

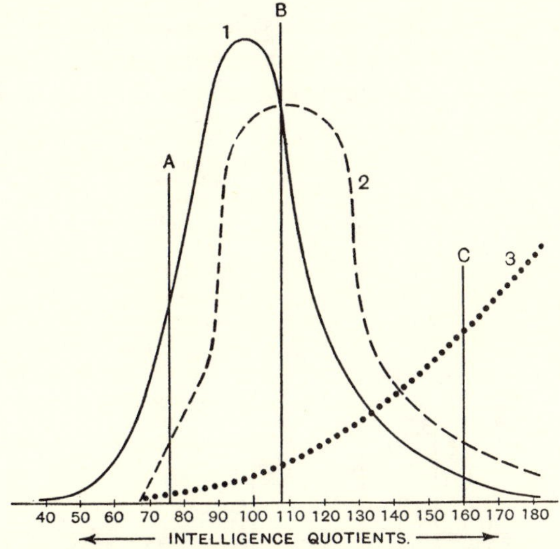

Fig. 1.[1] A. Supply greatly in excess of demand at 75 I.Q.—negligible wage. B. Supply and demand equal—normal wage. C. Demand greatly in excess of supply—disproportionate wage. (1) ——— Distribution of actual I.Q.'s. (2) – – – – Distribution of demand for I.Q.'s. (3) . . . . . . Rate of rewards arising from relation of (1) and (2).

intelligence distribution curve such as is caused by the present change in the curve of birth-rates would adjust to such a curve of demand. In stable, progressive conditions of civilization, on the other hand, such a change in the curve of supply must result in unemployment being greatest at the lower levels of intelligence.

In confirmation of this we may consider Fig. 2, showing the intelligence levels of children of unemployed in the two areas surveyed in the original research. It may be objected that in any period of unemployment it is only natural that the more intelligent will in competition secure jobs; but it is yet to be proven that these are too intelligent for the jobs they take.

[1] I am indebted to the *Eugenics Review* for permission to reproduce the diagrams shown in Figs. 1 and 2.

Students of population have long seen the errors of the naïve view that unemployment is due to overpopulation; next they have passed to studies of the economics of production and distribution; but it is possible that they will find at the root of the economic problem a psychological problem arising from the social effects of too great a range of innate individual differences in mental effectiveness.

Any attempt to discover the more direct effects upon wealth of changing intelligence levels must rest upon generalities. Recent work has shown a correlation of 0·9 to exist between the earning power of occupations and their mean intelligence demand (7). It has been argued

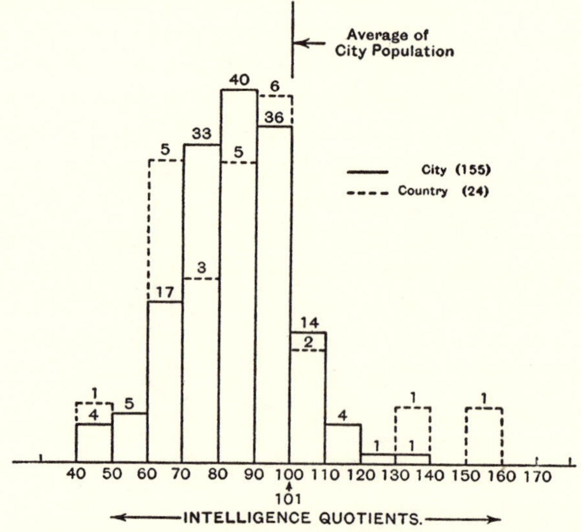

Fig. 2. Intelligence distribution of children of unemployed persons.

by some serious sociologists that the capacity to produce wealth is associated with inheritable mental attributes such as intelligence, but the facts of persistence of wealth in certain families may prove equally well an association of the capacity to seize property from others with inheritable or environmentally produced deficiency of character.

Nevertheless, it cannot be denied that the wealth of a community possessing a given quantity of raw material depends upon the quality and number of its inventive and organizing brains—and if inventive capacity is high enough, almost anything can become raw material. A decline in the numbers of high intelligence quotients must consequently mean a decline in the amount of goods and energy available for distribution in that community.

(*c*) *In moral standards*

The experiences of Child Guidance Clinics and the repetition in various parts of the world of the researches of Burt (1) and Healy (10) indicate that delinquent children are on an average of significantly lower intelligence than non-delinquent children from the same social stratum.

Among the probable causes of this connexion seem to be: (i) The duller child does not so easily foresee the consequences of his actions or the likelihood of detection. (ii) Low intelligence is associated with suggestibility to evil counsels. (iii) In a complex environment the less able child is less successful in finding the normal amount of self-expression for psychic energy. He is more frequently frustrated or exploited by others. He is, in general, more hard pressed by economic restriction. In short, he has to handle a greater load of suppression. (iv) Whilst he suffers from this greater curtailment of direct instinctive expression, he is at the same time less able to achieve satisfaction in alternative indirect expression; for adequate intelligence is a condition of satisfaction in sublimations through art, music, science, social service and the activities approved by civilization. (v) Since he is of low intelligence there is a statistical probability that he has been brought up by parents of low intelligence, who have followed inconsistent and short-sighted policies in character education.

The relative importance of each of these processes would be better understood if there were evidence as to whether delinquency is associated with absolute low intelligence, or merely with intelligence which is low relative to the average for the group.

If the latter, then a decrease in average intelligence, the scatter remaining constant, would not result in increased delinquency, for the tendency to delinquency is in proportion to the maladaptation of the lower ranges to the culture standards of the pervasive average. This argument, however, overlooks the fact, long pointed out by such psychologists as McDougall, that the crust of custom and tradition has a persistent life of its own, beyond that of the individuals creating the custom. Though the average of intelligence may fall, therefore, the standards of behaviour, discrimination and sublimation can be expected to persist for a generation or more, with only sporadic patches of decrepitude. It is the discrepancy between the level of this persisting culture and that of the mental capacity of the new generation of living individuals which is crucial to the development of delinquency.

Under delinquency we commonly think solely of delinquency against society, yet there are some forms of behaviour damaging to the individual and society which might be called delinquency against nature, for they arise from a mishandling of human dealings with nature. Such behaviour extends from the small child hurting himself because he refuses to recognize the physical properties of a chair to a society injuring itself through reckless use of an obviously limited supply of natural resources. In child-guidance work it is often very strikingly illustrated that the child whose stupid reactions bring him into excessive conflict with his fellows is also excessively scarred through accidents arising from a stupid handling of natural objects. This delinquency against nature involves the group as well as the individual; for the group suffers from the individual's excess of activity over judgment.

From such considerations it seems reasonable to conclude that delinquency as it is commonly understood—'delinquency against society'—is a function of the difference between the individual's intelligence and that of the average of the society to whose standards he is constrained; whereas delinquency in the wider sense—'delinquency against nature', resulting in any kind of damage to society and the individual—is a function of the absolute level of intelligence.

Owing to that persistence of culture habits described above, however, the fall in average intelligence which we are discussing would, in fact, result in an increase of both types of anti-social action. It would be interesting to know what part of the present increase in juvenile delinquency is attributable to intelligence distribution changes.

Throughout it has been the plan of this enquiry to confine the investigation to the direct psychological effects. Nevertheless it cannot be overlooked that these would often be powerfully accentuated or modified by simultaneous effects operating in other fields, e.g. the increase in economic divergence discussed above would increase the provocation to delinquency. The possible reciprocations of primary consequences, resulting in consequences of a second order, are too numerous to study here; but in the matter now being discussed there is a point of such interest that it would seem to justify departing from the condition that other things are equal, and following up the result of another social variable varying along with intelligence.

Above we have supposed that the demands of culture will persist at their present level. Although culture habits in their deeper levels have considerable persistence, there are times, e.g. at the birth of some new religious impulse, or the impact of one culture upon another, when few things can change more rapidly. It is possible, therefore, that instead of persisting the present restraints will either slacken, in response to the fall of intelligence, or that an attempt at over-compensation will be made by tightening up inhibitions to a hitherto unobtained level.

Before looking at the consequences of these alternatives, it is necessary to consider the ways in which instinctive expression is modified by culture. Generally the original biological goal of hunger, sex, gregariousness, etc., is maintained, being reached, however, by a longer circuit. Instead of hunting his food a man may earn it by working as a clerk. This involves a certain psychological strain and demands, generally, more intelligence than the original mode of behaviour. But instincts may even become what Freud has called 'aim inhibited', i.e. sublimated to some goal resembling but not as satisfying as the original biological goal. This renunciation demands 'plasticity' in the nervous system, a thing about which we know little, but generally it also requires intelligence, for the substitutes offered are generally of a complex kind.

Neither of these instinct changes is, in itself, better carried out by reason of good intelligence (unless it should be proved that 'plasticity' correlates with intelligence). Pascal is said to have responded to a disappointment in love by becoming increasingly entranced with the higher mathematics, and this sublimation is clearly not possible without such an intelligence as would make mathematics fascinating; but a feeble-minded person might respond equally well to the same situation, as in cases I have observed, by an interest in painting walls or smashing stones with a hammer. Similarly a man who doesn't get his food by the enjoyment of hunting may earn it, if he has a low I.Q., by turning a crank, with no more long-circuiting than occurs in the individual with a higher I.Q. who does the work of a clerk.

The chief reason, therefore, why the person of greater capacity is less delinquent and more able to tolerate either long-circuiting of instinct or its sublimation must be that civilization offers more opportunities for long-circuiting and sublimation at higher levels than at lower levels of complexity.

For all individuals some of the time, and some individuals all of the time, the psychological strain of these instinct modifications—which I shall call 'deflection strain'—must approach the limit of toleration, so that delinquency is threatened. This problem has been dealt with from one aspect by Freud in *Civilization and its Discontents*. From the present aspect we see that any marked fall of average intelligence with the same standard of culture is going to increase 'deflection strain' to an explosive pitch.

In individual psychology it frequently happens that free-floating emotion from unexpressed unconscious sources irrationally fastens itself upon some chance external object, or that unconscious attitudes are 'projected' upon innocent objects. The irritation engendered by the frustrations of 'deflection strain' may well be one of the main drives for acts of war, and for the projection of hostile attitudes upon foreign countries. A fall of intelligence in a civilization which retains its complexity in spite of the less adequate mentalities of its bearers may, therefore, be associated with an increased readiness to action which relieves the tension of 'deflection strain' by war.

The first solution of the 'deflection strain' arising from intelligence decline which is likely to appeal to a community conscious of its cause, would be a systematized relaxation of moral standards, permitting more direct instinctive satisfactions and harmless and culturally valueless long-circuitings. The widespread creation of easy amusements in the cinema, the radio and the best-seller novel show that this is going on to-day, and these institutions might cater for a fall in average intelligence in such a way as to handle 'deflection strain' without allowing any increase in delinquency. Economic measures might do the same, for 'deflection strain' is greater for low than for high intelligences under conditions of material deprivation. The substitution of lower for higher recreational values is, however, a moral loss to the community in the fullest sense of morality.

There remains the alternative of the community being provoked, as it were, by the threatened decline into an actual increase of restraints and the imposition of higher standards, such as might occur in a strongly religious society. Granted sterner inhibition the limits of deflection strain would then be indicated not by an increase in delinquency but by a mounting incidence of suicides, melancholiacs and perhaps neurotics generally. At the same time there would be a loss of expressiveness and *joie-de-vivre* throughout the community, with resultant changes in the creativity and in the general type of culture. To maintain the same percentage of delinquency with a falling intelligence average, therefore, it seems that the community must either invent substitute satisfactions at a low level or revert to Spartan or Puritanical standards of suppression.

(*d*) *In political and social life*

We are confining consideration in the main to consequences of a fall of intelligence, but the kind of change actually foreshadowed in the birth-rate survey described almost certainly includes also an increase in the standard deviation, principally through a relatively large increase in the 70–80 I.Q. range remote from the present mode.

The political consequences of such a change may be expected to arise directly through the increasing mental distance between individuals, and indirectly through changes in economic status brought about by the change. Outstanding among the latter would be the development of a larger 'social problem group' or at least of a group supported, supervised and patronized by extensive state social welfare work. Even if, through the supersession of *laissez-faire* by control of earnings, increased economic divergence were prevented, the direct 'distancing' effect would still persist: people may have uniform wage-rates and yet diverge greatly in social life and habits through differences in complexity of occupation, prestige and the presence or absence of intellectual interests. Any increase in the standard deviation is inimical to that human solidarity and potential equality of prestige which is essential to democracy.

Experimental evidence in the political field is slight but consistent. In three American Universities (14) where the students had already been tested for intelligence, a questionnaire permitting a rating on a Radical-Conservative scale and in which the political views were given adequate place, showed a significant relation between higher intelligence and more radical views. Other researches (8,11) confirm this relationship. Terman (16), having worked out from childhood records the I.Q.'s of eminent men in political life, afterwards sorted them into radical and conservative groups. The latter had the lower average intelligence.

Psychological analysis suggests that the above is not the whole story. To see all sides of a question, to make a discriminating and qualified, rather than an all-or-nothing response, requires higher intelligence. A fall of average mental capacity means an increase in the number of people capable of being led into extremist positions.

It is a commonplace in education that freedom can generally be safely given to a child in proportion to his intelligence. Newer systems of education, allowing the child considerable rights of self-determination, work admirably with gifted children; but at the other end of the scale, among border-line feeble-minded children in special classes, it is noticeable that children neither desire nor tolerate much individual freedom. It is as if, intuitively, or through experience, they realize that the greatest happiness of all concerned depends upon their being given rigid rules of conduct prescribing behaviour even to the extent of most detailed traditions and taboos. In social behaviour, as in arithmetic, they cannot safely be left to proceed far on their own.

Though the above relation of conservatism with lower intelligence has been described in the political field, the failure to appreciate reform or to desire the freedom to which reform will lead is shown equally, by the questionnaire study (8), to hold for progressiveness in the social field. Reformers during a generation suffering a falling average of intelligence will consequently experience greater difficulty in finding support for intelligent modification of obsolete, unadjusted habits and a slowing down of social change may therefore be expected.

The above considerations combined suggest the probability of political changes of a complex kind. They include lack of cohesion between social groups, together with changes of mental attitude such as might lead to the dissolution of the ideal of democracy; a decrease of the tempo of liberal progressiveness, an increase in those who pin their faith to simplified extremist formulae; and a hardening of rigid disciplines which preclude individual freedom.

(e) *In general culture*

There remain for discussion certain effects of a more general kind on the mental life of the group as a whole.

Among people exposed to much the same cultural influences, it is surprising how highly the amount of general information at the command of any individual is dependent upon mental capacity. Correlations of '*g*' with size of vocabulary, for example, are commonly as high as 0·8.

The smooth and efficient running of social life in a civilization of a complex kind, having many specialized institutions, requires a reasonably high level of general knowledge in all its members. Civilization is, after all, largely a body of knowledge—words, for example, do not live in dictionaries, but in the minds of writers—and people who cannot heed important parts of that background certainly cannot acquire the appropriate attitudes. Furthermore, any specialized question, affecting the life of the community as a whole, must be able to impinge upon a sufficient number and variety of alert people to ensure that the reaction is such as to be in the interests of the community as a whole. A decline in average intelligence means a shrinkage of the field of general knowledge which each person is capable of absorbing, and consequently a reduction in the number of people aware of anything but the simplest issues within the ambit of their daily lives. This must lead to an inertness of society and a dangerous slowness or lack of integration in responding to political and social dangers.

This problem has already been studied experimentally in the previous section with regard to politics; we may here look at it in a more general way. Any new idea appearing in a community can be reacted to by those who understand it either in a friendly or a hostile fashion. But the people who do not understand it will usually treat it in a hostile fashion. Every idea must have, according to its complexity, a certain percentage of the community capable of appreciating it. It can percolate downwards very rapidly so far but, reaching the larger stratum of people who understand it with difficulty, it moves very slowly and must depend for its progress upon emotional pressure and extraneous historical factors.

There is thus for every idea a certain I.Q. which may be called its 'demostatic level', down to which it may be fully understood, and an I.Q. stretch below that over which it has some lesser influence, which may be called its 'percolation range'.

Thus in the field of literary art Leavis (12) complains that "the rate at which *cultural* news penetrates is surprisingly slow...considering the elaborate machinery for disseminating such news which civilization possesses", and continues "the Book Clubs are instruments not for improving taste but for standardizing it at the middlebrow level, thus preventing the natural progression of taste that in the later eighteenth century, for instance, was assisted". The phenomenon would be explicable on the present hypothesis on the grounds that in the eighteenth century 'taste' had still not penetrated to its demostatic level, whereas to-day it has, and the maligned Book Clubs are only stabilizing each variety of taste at its most natural and stable level. The naïve supposition that progress of ideas downwards through society is continuous though slow, arises from the observation of slow movement in the 'percolation range'; but in fact no idea can get beyond its percolation range, and may be proceeding to an arrest at an I.Q. level which must be quite high in certain instances, e.g. the Special Theory of Relativity.

The vigour with which mental energy invests an idea or course of action is a function of the simplicity of the latter. Corresponding to the demostatic level and percolation range in society there is for each individual, in the range of ideas which assails him, an upper limit of easy comprehension ending in a point beyond which no further complexity can be handled at all. To the range beyond this point he can generally apply nothing but a passive hostility; to the middle range of dim comprehension he can give only weak support or criticism; to the lowest range he can give the full weight of his emotional life. Consequently the amount of energy available in society for any given idea must depend on the demostatic level for that idea and the percentage of people in the given community above that I.Q. level, plus a value obtained by multiplying the numbers in each level of the percolation range by a fraction which diminishes from one to zero in passing from the top to the bottom of the percolation range. This we may call the 'psychic energy investment' of the idea, and it will vary from community to community according to the average level of I.Q. and the distribution of I.Q.

Between any two minds in the same culture there is bound to be more or less overlap in knowledge, interests and sentiments. This we may call 'mental overlap', and upon its extent depends the amount of social cohesion in any purpose which may attract the energy of society. Good mental overlap does not ensure common purpose, but it is the necessary fruitful soil of common sympathy in which the latter may grow. A reduction of average mental capacity means a reduction of mental overlap in all minds and a failure of any mental overlap whatever in the socially, geographically and occupationally more remote minds; so that social cohesion, and the size of the group in which successful cohesion can be maintained, are diminished. Reduction of mental overlap arising from that diminution in the radius of individual minds produced by the substitution of lower for higher I.Q.'s thus has two major consequences:

(1) The impairment of social cohesion.

(2) Reduction in the intensity of cultural life, which is the sum of these overlaps, or, otherwise expressed, of the total psychic energy investment of a given set of ideas—the ideas which give form to that culture.

A similar process must take place within the limited fields of the special sciences and arts. The inability of what we regard as the intelligent person to cope with the increased complexity of modern culture has been met by accepting the device of specialization. Versatile minds, capable of taking all knowledge for their province, are far rarer to-day than in Elizabethan times; indeed it has begun to be considered presumption to attempt proficiency in more than one field of learning. Yet co-ordinating minds are always urgently needed, and the progress of one science often depends upon its being brought into relation with another. Either a further increase in accumulated but undigested information, or a decline of mental capacity in the workers serving those sciences, or both, would have the effect of bringing major progress to a halt and of preventing a synthesis of sciences either for the practical good of the community or for the attainment of truer philosophical perspectives.

The relation of intelligence to the type of interests, particularly social and recreational interests, must next be considered, for the latter react subtly yet strongly on the individual personality as a whole, and consequently upon the effectiveness of the individual as a member of society.

In a research in which children's preferences for various tests were studied, the present writer found that the obtained order of preference was practically the reverse of the order of '*g*' saturation (3). Above a certain modest intelligence demand the occupations were most liked which demanded least use of intelligence. The same is found with school subjects; the brilliant child may prefer English or Mathematics, both highly '*g*' saturated, but the dull child takes a natural interest principally in handwork, games and simple repetitive tasks.

In the recent research on popular reading habits, mentioned above (12), the literary student scornfully compares the standard of the accepted newspaper of 1850 with that of to-day, adding some scathing comments on fifty years of free and compulsory education. But, as indicated in the discussion on demostatic level, the difference is far more simply explained as being due to the increased social range in the reading public, necessarily accompanied by an increased percentage of readers from the lower ranges of the intelligence distribution curve, a change equivalent to a decline in the average mental capacity of the reading public. Even so the decline in standards might not have occurred without the newspaper magnates' devotion to "supplying the public with what it wants". But had this not been done on commercial grounds it would have been done on grounds of freedom; indeed in most fields of recreation it is in any case impossible to prevent people doing the things for which their level of intelligence best fits them. It is a short-lived mistake to force Aldous Huxley on people who want all-in wrestling, or Beethoven on those who can only enjoy the crudest of cinema drama.

When coercion by schoolmaster and highbrow ceases, as it is ceasing, because of its fruitlessness, a more subtle kind of coercion in the reverse direction will have to be taken into account. Comparing the tone of the Press in America and in this country, H. G. Wells has cautioned us that there are no more fools in America than in Great Britain. It is only that they are more vocal there.

Once free expression is conceded it is clear that the type which constitutes the mode of the intelligence distribution is going to become the most loudly expressed. Owing to the emotional force of the gregarious instinct and the wear and tear which the individual constantly suffers in trying to detach his reactions from those of the dominant average, the modes of expression of the more intelligent are always constrained towards those of that average. Without a sharper splitting of the social life of intellectual classes this is inevitable, and since intellectual classification is not the same as social classification, being less organized, only societies based on special interests keep the rarer interests alive.

These psychological forces quickly bring in their train material and economic associates. Thus when publishing becomes a purely commercial proposition, no publisher is likely to take on a 'highbrow' author with small circulation when he can employ a 'best-seller' author. The more widely used commodity actively pushes that desired by a few people off the market, whether that minority happens to be merely eccentric or culturally important.

Some alienation of the recreational and cultural interests of various classes may well occur if we continue to facilitate, through equalization of opportunity, the sorting out of classes according to intelligence, and if the natural variability of intelligence is at the same time increased through the present birth-rate trends. In any case the fall in the I.Q. level of the mode itself must result in a significant impoverishment and stultification of the cultural life of the average and the superior.

Finally we have to consider a general change towards which many primary and secondary changes are working. We have seen that there must be some decline in the cultural level attained by education, and some arrest in economic progress. To these effects must be added a decrease within the community as a whole of qualities of foresight and resistance to suggestibility, for deficiency in these is particularly characteristic of persons of defective intelligence (15).[1]

Increasing deflection strain not alleviated by any deliberate or accidental lowering of cultural demands may be reacted to, as we have seen, either by individual delinquency or war. But since all the above changes in education and economics, the diminished foresight and increased suggestibility, are such as to produce minor or major internal or external sufferings or calamities, the course of history may well lead

[1] An academic acquaintance, visiting the dentist remarked, "seeing a dentist before a tooth hurts is an act of pure intelligence", and though foresight is a conative rather than a cognitive quality it undoubtedly correlates with intelligence.

to adjustment by way of increased inhibition rather than by way of appropriate reduction of deflection strain.

In that case two responses are possible; either the traditional reaction to frustration by religious emotion and observance or the newer expression of thwartings through the phantasy of the novel and the cinema. This phantasy expression is to-day reaching tremendous dimensions, and we have probably not seen the end of its development or begun to appreciate its damaging effects on 'reality thinking' habits concerned in other spheres of life.

As regards the increase in a religious type of adaptation, it is clear that the trend of rationalist education may be powerfully against this, but the increased conservatism, suggestibility and limitation of mental range are in its favour. And rationalist notions, at least constructive rationalist notions attempting to give a philosophic conception of life in keeping with all the established findings of modern science, are bound quickly to reach their demostatic level, whereas the cruder symbolisms and approximations to the same truths contained in religion will readily acquire, owing to the bulge in the lower ranges of the I.Q. distribution curve, a far higher psychic investment energy. The imponderables, especially in this final calculation, are too many to justify the statement that a back-to-religion movement in the conventional sense of religion is probable, but the rough draft of a formula for the social response to an I.Q. decline can at least be given, and one possible solution of it is clearly an increase in religious forms of self-expression.

V. Summary

This thesis, elaborated partly on experimental and partly on analytical grounds, indicates that the probable consequences of a downward shift in the intelligence distribution curve are as follows:

1. A fall in academic standards in the schools.
2. A change in the curriculum of schools towards less abstract and generalized studies.
3. An increased cost of education.
4. Increased unemployment in the less-skilled occupations.
5. Decrease in the average real earning capacity of the community as a whole.
6. A rise in the frequency of delinquency (unless there is a deliberate lowering of moral standards) or/and proneness to aggression between nations.

7. Alternatively, if inhibitory forces prevail, either (*a*) an increase in the social equipment provided for phantasy compensations, or (*b*) an increase in religious expression.

8. An increase in the percentage of people adopting extreme or uncompromising political view-points, together with the growth of a generally conservative position.

9. An increased retardation in the percolation of 'cultural news', together with a lowering of the intensity of cultural life and a diminution in the rate of scientific discoveries and other specialized advances.

10. A shift of cultural and recreational interests to cruder tastes and forms of expression, together with an increased divergence of interest between different groups and a greater domination by the average.

11. A check to the growth of social and political freedom and a reversion to a more detailed prescription of individual behaviour.

REFERENCES

(1) Burt, C. (1925). *The Young Delinquent.* London: University of London Press.

(2) Cattell, R. B. (1931). "The assessment of teaching ability." *Brit. J. educ. Psychol.* I, 48.

(3) Cattell, R. B. & Bristol, H. (1933). "Intelligence tests for mental ages of 4–8 years." *Brit. J. educ. Psychol.* III, 142.

(4) Cattell, R. B. (1934). "Occupational norms of intelligence, and the standardization of an adult intelligence test." *Brit. J. Psychol.* XXV, 1.

(5) —— (1936). "Is national intelligence declining?" *Eugenics Review*, XXVIII, 3.

(6) —— (1937). *The Fight for Our National Intelligence.* London: P. S. King.

(7) —— (1937). "Some further relations between intelligence, fertility and socio-economic status." *Eugenics Review*, XXIX, 3.

(8) Eckert, R. E. (1935). "Analysing the superior college student." *School and Soc.* XLI, 69.

(9) Gray, J. L. & Moskinsky, P. (1935). "Ability and opportunity in English education." *Sociol. Rev.*, XXVII, 113.

(10) Healy, T. (1920). *The Individual Delinquent.* Chicago.

(11) Howells, T. H. (1929). "A study of religious orthodoxy." *Univ. Iowa, Service Bull.* XIII, No. 38.

(12) Leavis, Q. D. (1932). *Fiction and the Reading Public.* London: Chatto and Windus.

(13) Miles, G. H. (1937). "Fatigue from the industrial point of view." *The Human Factor*, XI, 8.

(14) Murphy, G. *et al.* (1937). *Experimental Social Psychology.* New York: Harper.

(15) Porteus, S. D. & Babcock, M. E. (1926). *Temperament and Race.* Boston.

(16) Terman, L. M. (1925). *Genetic Studies of Genius*, vol. I. California: Stanford University Press.